UNL⌀CK

BASIC LITERACY

Emma Pathare and Gary Pathare

CAMBRIDGE
UNIVERSITY PRESS

CAMBRIDGE
UNIVERSITY PRESS

University Printing House, Cambridge CB2 8BS, United Kingdom

One Liberty Plaza, 20th Floor, New York, NY 10006, USA

477 Williamstown Road, Port Melbourne, VIC 3207, Australia

4843/24, 2nd Floor, Ansari Road, Daryaganj, Delhi – 110002, India

79 Anson Road, #06–04/06, Singapore 079906

Cambridge University Press is part of the University of Cambridge.

It furthers the University's mission by disseminating knowledge in the pursuit of education, learning and research at the highest international levels of excellence.

www.cambridge.org
Information on this title: www.cambridge.org/9781316636466

© Cambridge University Press 2017

First published 2017

20 19 18 17 16 15 14 13 12 11 10 9 8 7 6 5 4 3 2 1

Printed in Italy by Rotolito Lombarda S.p.A.

A catalogue record for this publication is available from the British Library

ISBN 978-1-316-63646-6 Unlock Basic Literacy Student's Book with Downloadable Audio
ISBN 978-1-316-63645-9 Unlock Basic Skills Student's Book with Downloadable Audio and Video
ISBN 978-1-316-63649-7 Unlock Basic Literacy Teacher's Book with Downloadable Audio
ISBN 978-1-316-63648-0 Unlock Basic Skills Teacher's Book with Downloadable Audio and Video

CONTENTS

UNIT	LITERACY AND HANDWRITING	LISTENING AND READING	KEY WORDS FOR LITERACY
STARTER	Greetings, numbers, classroom instructions, the alphabet, consonant sounds and vowel sounds		
1 MEETING PEOPLE	Capital letters for names and countries Spelling names Writing numbers 0–10 (digits) **ACADEMIC WRITING SKILLS:** Punctuation: full stops and question marks **SPELLING CHALLENGE:** Words with *a, e, i, o* and *u*	Understanding personal questions Reading an email	Focus on *he, she, you, the*
2 PEOPLE AND THINGS	Writing: *Mr, Mrs, Dr*; short verb forms with an apostrophe, numbers 0–10 (words), numbers 11–100 (digits and words) **ACADEMIC WRITING SKILLS:** Punctuation: capital letters at the start of a sentence Full stops **SPELLING CHALLENGE:** Focus on *date, lime, cape* and *pipe*	Understanding details about objects and people Reading a description of a class	Focus on *are, is, one, two, from*
3 UNIVERSITY LIFE	Capital letters for subjects Capital letters for days of the week Spelling words **ACADEMIC WRITING SKILLS:** Joining sentences with *and* Punctuation: question marks, full stops and commas **SPELLING CHALLENGE:** Focus on *home, student, perfume, hole, globe* and *dune*	Understanding questions about subjects people study Reading an email	Focus on *it, at, in, on*
4 DIFFERENT COUNTRIES	Spelling words Capital letters for countries and cities **ACADEMIC WRITING SKILLS:** Joining sentences with *and* Punctuation: breaking a longer text into sentences Commas **SPELLING CHALLENGE:** Focus on *teacher, desert, jeep, beach, family* and *sea*	Listening to short introductions of places Reading short descriptions of countries and cities	Focus on *what, who, when, where*
5 WORK	Spelling of jobs Verbs with *s* for *he* and *she* in Present simple Capital letters for months **ACADEMIC WRITING SKILLS:** Recognising verbs in sentences Punctuation: capital letters Full stops at the end of a sentence **SPELLING CHALLENGE:** Focus on *cries, washes, flies* and *watches*	Understanding information about people's jobs Reading a poster with details	Focus on *with, we, work, write*

WRITING	LANGUAGE	PRONUNCIATION
Complete sentences with personal information. **WRITING CHALLENGE**: Write about you. Complete sentences with *his*, *her*, *number* and *first*. Write about your teacher.	**Vocabulary**: ID, countries, study objects **Grammar**: Possessive adjectives The verb *be*	Word stress **SOUND AND SPELLING**: *p, b* Short vowels
Write about your class. **WRITING CHALLENGE**: Write about a person in your family. Write about two teachers. Write about your family.	**Vocabulary**: Family, my things, numbers 11–100 **Grammar**: The verb *be*: *we* and *they* Possessive adjectives (*our*, *their*) Regular plural nouns	**SOUND AND SPELLING**: *th* Word stress Silent *e – a_e, i_e*
Complete a timetable. Write about your timetable. **WRITING CHALLENGE**: Write about you. Write about a subject.	**Vocabulary**: Subjects, days of the week, adjectives, time **Grammar**: *When/where* and *in/on/at* The verb *be*: *it*	Word stress **SOUND AND SPELLING**: *sh, ch, th* Silent *e – o_e, u_e*
Make notes about a country, city and place. Write about your country and a city in your country. **WRITING CHALLENGE**: Write about your country. Write about a city in your country.	**Vocabulary**: Describing countries, describing cities, *Wh-* questions **Grammar**: Prepositions *in* and *from* The verb *be*: negative	Word stress **SOUND AND SPELLING**: *e, ee, ea* *Wh-* sounds
Write about your friend. **WRITING CHALLENGE**: Write about a person. Write about your day.	**Vocabulary**: Jobs, my day, work, months **Grammar**: Article *a* Preposition *at* Preposition *in* with months Present simple affirmative: *he* and *she*	Word stress **SOUND AND SPELLING**: *f, ph, ff* Adding *s* *ou*

UNIT	LITERACY AND HANDWRITING	LISTENING AND READING	KEY WORDS FOR LITERACY
6 FOOD AND HEALTH	Spelling of words describing food and drink *ACADEMIC WRITING SKILLS*: Avoiding repetition by using pronouns Finding and correcting mistakes *SPELLING CHALLENGE*: Words with *ee*, *ea* and *i*	Listening to a survey Reading an academic statistical article	Focus on *of, some, lot, not*
7 PLACES	Spelling of: words describing places, phrases, plural nouns *ACADEMIC WRITING SKILLS*: Completing sentences with adjectives Completing sentences with prepositions *SPELLING CHALLENGE*: Focus on *start, park, airport* and *work* Focus on *train, station, street* and *student*	Understanding information about places in the city Reading a university website	Focus on *new, old, between, to*
8 SPENDING	Spelling of objects Writing large numbers (digits and words) *ACADEMIC WRITING SKILLS*: Word order in sentences Punctuation: full stops and question marks Completing sentences with frequency words *SPELLING CHALLENGE*: Focus on *day, games, train, pay* and *newspaper*	Understanding information about people's spending habits Reading a business report	Focus on *buy, by, have, and*
9 TECHNOLOGY	Spelling of words describing technology, regular and irregular plural nouns *ACADEMIC WRITING SKILLS*: Joining sentences with *but* Punctuation: full stops and commas *SPELLING CHALLENGE*: Focus on *plays, glasses* and *blog* Focus on *fridge* and *watch*	Listening to a debate on technology Reading an article on using technology	Focus on *can, never, often, always*
10 FREE TIME AND FASHION	Spelling of words describing free-time activities *ACADEMIC WRITING SKILLS*: Joining sentences with *and, but* and *also* *SPELLING CHALLENGE*: Focus on *watch, student, drink* and *lunch*	Understanding information about people's free time and favourite colours and clothes Reading a blog with people's likes and dislikes	Focus on *this, these, they, their*

WRITING	LANGUAGE	PRONUNCIATION
Complete notes as preparation for writing. Write about your friend. **WRITING CHALLENGE**: Write about your friend. Write about your country.	*Vocabulary*: Food, daily routine, health, feelings *Grammar*: *don't* and *doesn't* *A lot of, some, not a lot of*	Word stress **SOUND AND SPELLING**: Review *ea, i, e, ee* *nk, st, nch*
Write about a famous place in your city. **WRITING CHALLENGE**: Write about your city. Write about your city in your country.	*Vocabulary*: Places in the city 1, places in the city 2, famous places, location *Grammar*: Article *a* and *an* *There is / There are* Adjectives	Word stress **SOUND AND SPELLING**: *rt, rk* Review *st, tr, str*
Write about your friend. **WRITING CHALLENGE**: Write about your friend. Write about your shopping.	*Vocabulary*: Things we buy, calendar time, shopping, money *Grammar*: Frequency expressions Present simple: questions	Word stress **SOUND AND SPELLING**: *ay, a_e, ai* *nd, ng*
Complete notes as preparation for writing. Write about your friend. **WRITING CHALLENGE**: Write about you. Write about a smart TV.	*Vocabulary*: Computers and the internet, things we use, people, asking for and giving opinions *Grammar*: *can* and *can't* (for possibility) Frequency expressions 2	Word stress **SOUND AND SPELLING**: Review *bl, pl, gl* *dge, tch*
Complete a survey as preparation for writing. Write an email. **WRITING CHALLENGE**: Write about your free time. Write about your friend.	*Vocabulary*: Free time, free time review, clothes, colours *Grammar*: Order of adjectives *Like + -ing* *This is / These are* Possessive *'s*	Word stress **SOUND AND SPELLING**: Review *-ing*

UNLOCK BASIC LITERACY

Unlock Basic Literacy is tailor-made for Arabic speakers and provides your students with extra support in:

- left-to-right reading and writing that recycles the language from *Unlock Basic Skills*
- handwriting with tracing exercises, writing lines and extra space to write
- sound and spelling informed by research into learner errors
- key words for literacy informed by research into the academic language students use.

UNL⌀CK BASIC LITERACY UNIT STRUCTURE

The units in *Unlock Basic Literacy* are carefully scaffolded so that students build the skills and language they need throughout the unit in order to cope successfully with the final Listening and Writing task.

LISTENING AND READING 1 **LISTENING AND READING 2** **LISTENING AND READING 3**	Provides information about the topic, introduces new vocabulary in context and focuses on the handwriting of these words. It practises listening and reading skills. Where relevant, this lesson also includes a focus on Sound and spelling which will further enhance literacy skills and listening and speaking comprehension. It contains Writing challenge sections and a Spelling challenge section.
LANGUAGE FOCUS	Practises the vocabulary and grammar from Listening and Reading 1-3, focuses on functional language and pre-teaches the vocabulary and grammar needed for the final Listening and Writing tasks. This lesson also includes a full-page Sound and spelling section.
LISTENING FOCUS	Features a listening text in an academic context that practises listening skills. It uses the language learnt over the course of the unit.
KEY WORDS FOR LITERACY	Features a list of carefully selected, high frequency and often problematic words. It provides students with an opportunity to practise these in detail with the aim of achieving automatic recognition.
READING AND WRITING	Features a reading text in an academic context, practises reading skills and acts as a model for the final writing task that uses the skills and language learnt over the course of the unit.

UNLOCK RESEARCH

UNLOCK BASIC ADVISORY PANEL

Unlock Basic has been developed in collaboration with the *Unlock Basic* Advisory Panel, expert teachers experienced in teaching pre-A1 level EAP students, so we can be sure the course meets your students' needs.

THE CAMBRIDGE CORPUS

Unique research using the **Cambridge English Corpus, the Cambridge Learner Corpus and English Profile** has been carried out to ensure the language provided is the right level and relevant to learners' studies. Our exclusive insights into official Cambridge English exam papers enable us to identify the most common errors that Arabic learners make and provide focussed practice material to give them support where they need it most.

| | | | MEETING PEOPLE | UNIT 1 |

⊙ KEY WORDS FOR LITERACY

1 🔊 1.11 Listen, read and (circle).

1	**he**	Where is (he) from? (He)'s from Bahrain.
2	**she**	She's from India. She's a teacher.
3	**you**	Where are you from?
4	**the**	He's from the UK. She's from the UAE.

2 Read and (circle).

1	**he**	→	her	→	hi	→	he	→	here	→	he
2	**she**	→	she	→	he's	→	shed	→	she	→	he
3	**you**	→	your	→	you	→	young	→	you	→	yours
4	**the**	→	the	→	there	→	the	→	het	→	them

3 Cover and complete.

UNLOCK BASIC

COURSE COMPONENTS

- *Unlock Basic* consists of two Student's Books: *Unlock Basic Skills & Unlock Basic Literacy* and an accompanying Teacher's Book for each.
- Complete course audio is available to download from esource.cambridge.org using the activation codes inside the front cover of the Student's Book.
- The *Unlock* Teacher's Books contain step-by-step lesson plans, additional activities, common student errors and teaching tips.
- Unit Review Tests, mid-level and end-of-level tests are available to download from esource.cambridge.org using the activation codes inside the front cover of the Teacher's Book.
- *Presentation Plus* **software for interactive whiteboards** is available for both Student's Books.

LISTENING
AND
SPEAKING

READING
AND
WRITING

HANDWRITING

1 👁 Look.

2 ✏ Trace.

3 ✏ Trace.

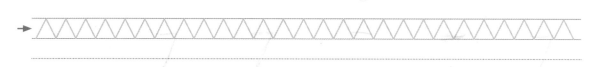

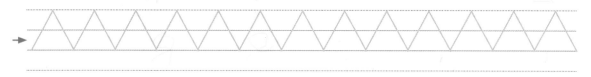

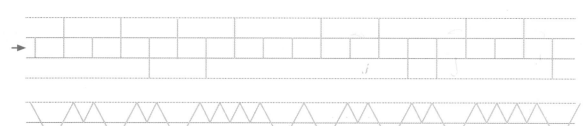

SPEAKING AND LISTENING **Hi. Hello. I'm ...**

1 🔊 0.1 👂 Listen.

2 🔊 0.2 👂 Listen.

3 🔊 0.3 👂 🗨 Listen and say.

 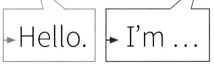

READING Numbers 0–10

1 🔊 0.4 👂 👉 Listen and point.

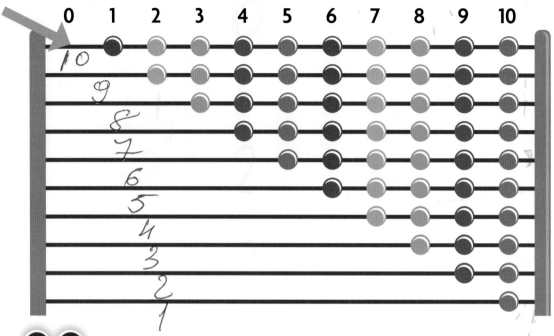

2 👁 🔤 Look and match.

6   8   2   5   10

3 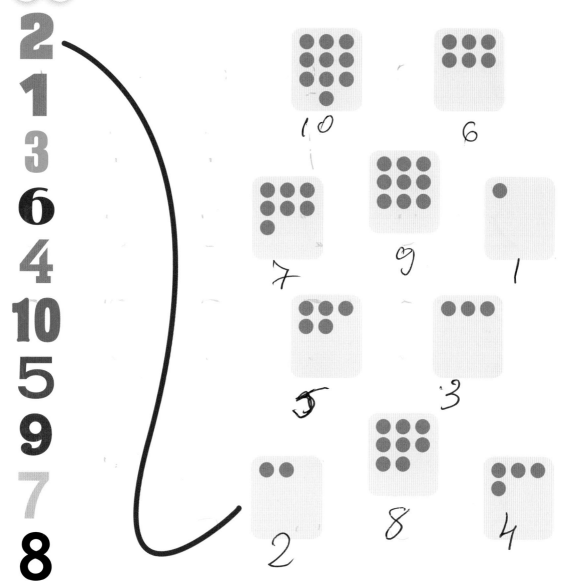 Look and match.

2
1
3
6
4
10
5
9
7
8

10   6

7   9   1

5   3

2   8   4

LISTENING AND SPEAKING Numbers 0–10

1 🔊 0.5 👂 👆 👁 Listen, point and say.

| 4 | 3 | 9 | 0 | 7 | 1 | 10 | 5 | 2 | 8 | 6 |

2 🔊 0.6 👂 👆 👁 Listen, point and say.

→ 0 → 1 → 2 → 3 → 4 → 5 → 6 → 7 → 8 → 9 → 10

WRITING Numbers 0–10

1 👁 ✏ Look and trace.

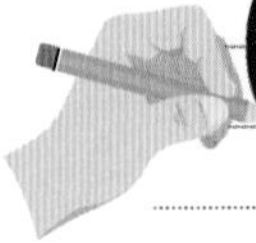

0 0 0 0 0 0 0

1 1 1 1 1 1 1

2 2 2 2 2 2 2

3 3 3 3 3 3 3

4 4 4 4 4 4 4

5 5 5 5 5 5 5

6 6 6 6 6 6 6

7 7 7 7 7 7 7

8 8 8 8 8 8 8

9 9 9 9 9 9 9

10 10 10 10 10 10

2 🔊 0.7 ✏️ 👂 🗣️ Write. Then listen and say.

10

3

5

7

0

2

4

6

1

8

9

3 🔊 0.8 👂 👁️ ✏️ Listen, look and write.

3

3

1

1

1

1

LISTENING AND READING **Instructions**

1 🔊 0.9 👂 👆 👁 Listen and point. Then say.

→ listen *1*　　→ say *2*　　→ read *3*

→ write *4*　　→ look *5*　　→ point *6*

2 🔊 0.10 👂 a–b c–a Listen and match.

1 → listen　　　　　　**2** → say

3 → read　　　　　　**4** → write

5 → look　　　　　　**6** → point

3 🔊 0.11 👂 ✏ Listen and write.

READING a–z

1 🔊 0.12 Listen and point.

→ a → b → c → d → e → f → g → h → i → j → k → l → m
→ n → o → p → q → r → s → t → u → v → w → x → y → z

2 🔊 0.13 Listen and say.

3 🔊 0.14 Look and (circle). Then listen and check. Write.

→ **a**   ⓐ e ⓐ o ⓐ | 3 |

→ **e**   o e a e o | |

→ **i**   i l t i j | |

→ **o**   a o a a e | |

→ **u**   u n v n u | |

4 🔊 0.15 Say. Then listen and check.

a e i o u

5 🔊 0.16 Look and (circle). Then listen and check. Write.

→ **p**   ⓟ q b p g d | |

→ **q**   g q p g q q | |

→ **b**   h d b b h b | |

→ **d**   q d b p d g | |

→ **g**   g p q g d p | |

→ **h**   b h d h g p | |

6 Match.

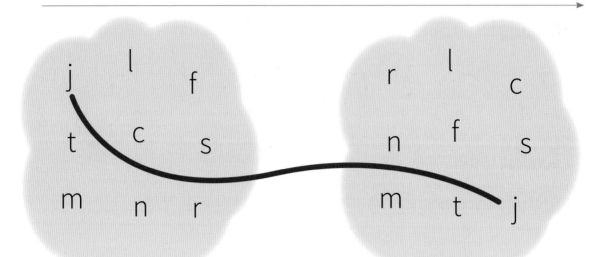

7 Match.

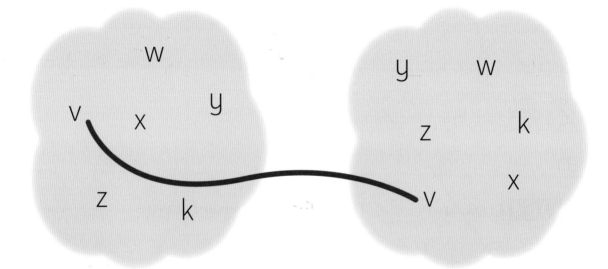

8 🔊 **0.17** Say. Then listen and check.

→ **1** **s→a→y**   **2** **r→e→a→d**

→ **3** **p→o→i→n→t**   **4** **w→r→i→t→e**

→ **5** **l→o→o→k**   **6** **l→i→s→t→e→n**

WRITING a–z

1 Trace.

2 🔊 0.18 Listen and say. Then write.

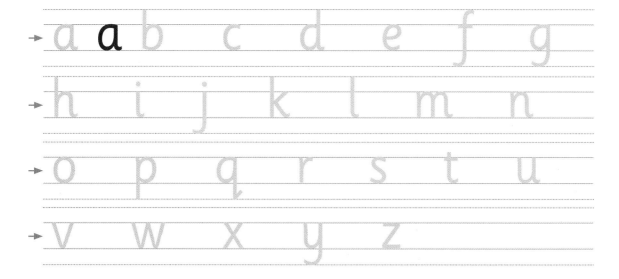

READING A–Z

1 🔊 0.19 Listen, point and say.

→ A ▸ B ▸ C ▸ D ▸ E ▸ F ▸ G ▸ H ▸ I ▸ J ▸ K ▸ L ▸ M

→ N ▸ O ▸ P ▸ Q ▸ R ▸ S ▸ T ▸ U ▸ V ▸ W ▸ X ▸ Y ▸ Z

2 🔊 0.20 Look and (circle). Then listen and check. Write.

→ **A**   N   Ⓐ   E   H   Ⓐ   H   V | 2 |

→ **E**   B   E   F   E   B   E   C | |

→ **I**   I   J   T   L   I   I   T | |

→ **O**   D   O   U   D   O   C   C | |

→ **U**   V   U   J   U   O   D   C | |

3 🔊 0.21 Look and (circle). Then listen and check. Write.

→ **C**   Ⓒ   S   D   C   G   C | |

→ **D**   D   Q   C   D   G   D | |

→ **Q**   G   Q   C   Q   D   C | |

→ **G**   Q   G   D   G   C   S | |

→ **S**   C   S   G   G   S   S | |

4 Match.

5 Match.

6 Look, match and (circle).

→ **1**    L E D F X S J I T

→ **2**    C D G O C

→ **3**    B S D F T D O B P

→ **4**   J L C T D O G P I L M N

7 🔊 0.22 Look and say. Then listen and check.

KSA   UAE   PC   UK

CD   BMW   ATM

WRITING A–Z

1 Trace.

2 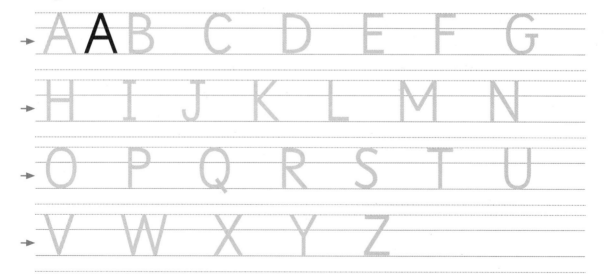 0.23 Listen and say. Then write.

WRITING Aa–Zz

1 Trace and write.

A a   A a   A a

B b   B b   B b

C c   C car   C cor

D d   D di   D di

E e   E e   E e

F f   F f   F f

G g   G gci   G gei

H h   H hoi   H hoi

I i   I i   I i

J j   J j   J j

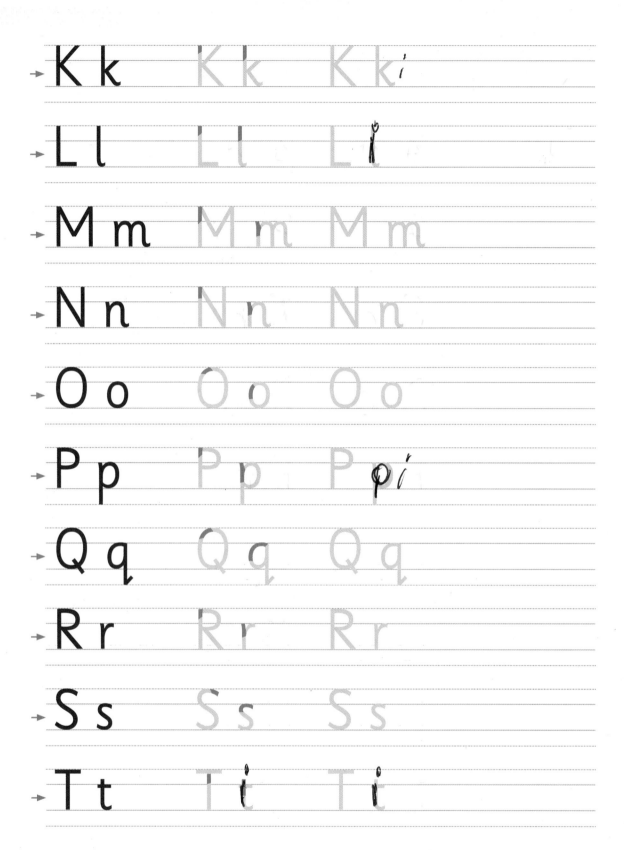

Kk   Kk   Kki

Ll   Ll   Li

Mm   Mm   Mm

Nn   Nn   Nn

Oo   Oo   Oo

Pp   Pp   Ppi

Qq   Qq   Qq

Rr   Rr   Rr

Ss   Ss   Ss

Tt   Ti   Ti

U u   U u   U u

V v   V v   V v

W w   W w   W w

X x   X x   X x

Y y   Y y   Y y

Z z   Z z   Z z

2 Look and write.

A a B b c D e F

g

3 Trace.

→ Aai Bis Ctji Di Ee Ef Gcith Hi Jt

→ Ki Li Mm Nn Oo Pi gy Ri Si

→ Fi Un Vi ww Xx Yu Zt

4 🔊 0.24 Write. Then listen.

→ Aai Bi Cc Dj Ee Ff Gi Hh Ii Jj

→ Ki Li Mm Nn Oo Pi Qq Rr Si Ti

→ Uu Vv Ww Xx Yr Zz

5 Look. Then copy.

→ cti Fi yr n Cinai bi qu hi M pi ki

→ ▢▢▢ F▢▢▢▢▢ ▢▢▢

6 🔊 0.25 Listen and write.

→ Ki Mn

SOUND AND SPELLING Consonants

1 🔊 0.26 Look, listen and say. Then trace.

 **b b**us
bus

 c coffee
coffee

 d doctor
doctor

 f four
four

 g gas
gas

 h hello
hello

 j jeans
jeans

 k kilogram
kilogram

 l lemon
lemon

 m message
message

 n nine
nine

 p palm
palm

 q queen
queen

 r radio
radio

 s salad
salad

 t ten
ten

 v video
video

 w Wi-Fi
Wi-Fi

 x ta**x**i
taxi

 **y y**acht
yacht

 z zero
zero

2 🔊 0.27 Listen, write and trace. Then listen and say.

g   p   W   r   ~~b~~   k   q   j

→ b us

→ alm

→ ueen

→ as

→ eans

→ ilogram

→ adio

→ i-Fi

3 🔊 0.28 Write and trace. Listen and check. Say.

s   h   z   n   v   ~~f~~   t

→ **4** f our

→ ello

→ **9** ine

→ alad

→ **10** en

→ ideo

→ **0** ero

UNLOCK BASIC LITERACY

SOUND AND SPELLING Vowels

1 🔊 0.29 Listen, look and (circle).

→ **a** g@s   palm

→ **o** coffee   hello

→ **e** lemon   zero

→ **u** bus

→ **i** video   Wi-Fi

READING AND WRITING Numbers zero–ten

1 🔊 0.30 Look and trace. Then listen and say.

●   ●●   ●●●   ●●●●   ●●●●●

→ **zero**   **one**   two   three   four   five

→ six   seven   eight   nine   ten

2 🔊 0.31 Match. Then listen and check.

one   three   nine   zero   eight

8   0   3   1   9

UNIT 1   MEETING PEOPLE

LISTENING AND READING 1

1 🔊 **1.1** Listen and read. Then match.

►Hi. I'm
►Jamal.

►Hello. I'm
►Hassan.

►Hi. I'm
►Nasser.

►Hello. I'm
►Amal.

►Hi. I'm
►Hessa.

Nasser ☐   Amal ☐   Hassan ☐   Jamal 1   Hessa ☐

2 🔊 **1.2** Listen, read and circle.

Aa ⟶ Asma Al Jawa   Bb ⟶ Badir Al Kaabi
Dd ⟶ Rowdah Al Digaishi   Hh ⟶ Hessa Al Hashimi
Nn ⟶ Nasser Al Ghanim   Rr ⟶ Rashid Al Faris

3 Trace the CAPITAL letters.

Nasser **A**l **G**hanim

1 Ahmed   2 Tariq

3 Sara   4 Hind

5 Al Kaabi   6 Al Qubaisi

NOTICE ❗
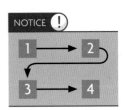

4 🔊 1.3 Listen and write the CAPITAL letters.

__ adir __ l __ aris   __ essa __ l __ awa   __ owdah __ l __ aabi

5 🔊 1.4 Listen and read. Then trace.

Hello. I'm Aisha.

How do you spell that?

A – i – s – h – a .

Hi. My name's Nasser.

How do you spell that?

N – a – double s – e – r .

6 🔊 1.5 Listen and circle the double letters.
Then say.

1 Moha mm ed
2 Abdullah
3 Ameena
4 Hessa
5 Shamma
6 Al Zaabi

NOTICE !

→ Nasser = N – a – double s – e – r
→ Hammad = H – a – double m – a – d

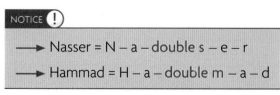

M – o – h – a – double m – e – d

7 🔊 **1.6** Listen, read and write.

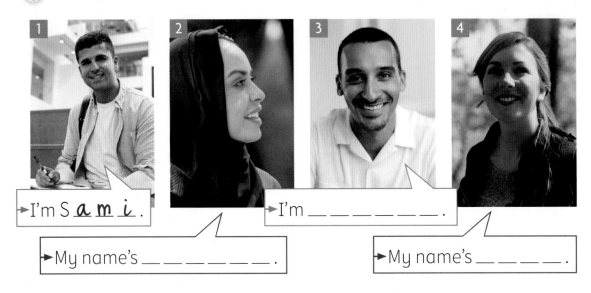

▸I'm S **a m i** .

▸I'm _ _ _ _ _ _ _ _ .

▸My name's _ _ _ _ _ _ _ _ .

▸My name's _ _ _ _ _ _ .

8 Read and write ▎.▕ or ▎?▕.

1 My name's Noora ▁•

2 I'm Rashid __

3 How do you spell that __

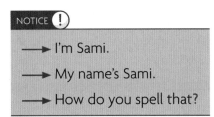

NOTICE ❗

⟶ I'm Sami.

⟶ My name's Sami.

⟶ How do you spell that?

9 🔊 **1.7** Find the words. Then listen and check.

1 My|name|is|Saud|Al|Faris.

2 IamAmeenaAlGhanim.

3 MynameisRosaGolijan.

4 Howdoyouspellthat?

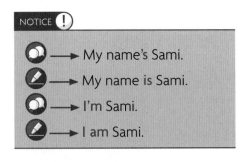

NOTICE ❗

🔊 ⟶ My name's Sami.

✏ ⟶ My name is Sami.

🔊 ⟶ I'm Sami.

✏ ⟶ I am Sami.

10 Writing Challenge Write about you.

My name is Khalid Al Faris.

LISTENING AND READING 2

1 🔊 1.8 Listen and write. Then say.

| 9 | 3 | 7 | 10 | 8 | 5 | 4 | 6 |

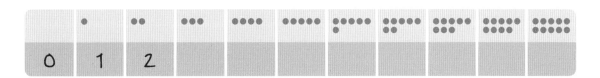

| 0 | 1 | 2 | | | | | | | | |

2 🔊 1.9 Listen and match.

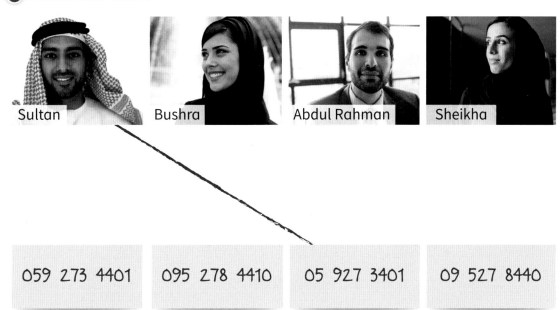

Sultan   Bushra   Abdul Rahman   Sheikha

059 273 4401   095 278 4410   05 927 3401   09 527 8440

3 🔊 1.10 Listen and correct.

1 Mehmet   039 28~~3~~ 946~~1~~
                   2   0

2 Abdul Aziz   0191 285 2875

3 Fatima   07806 428 926

4 Latifa   01273 805 157

4 Read and write . or ? .

1 What is your name ?

2 My name is Mohammed __

3 What is your number __

4 My number is 0997 0880 433 __

5 🔊 **1.11** Read and match. Listen and check.

1	**UNIVERSITY OF CAMBRIDGE**

STUDENT ID CARD

First name: **Ahmad**
Family name: **Al Kaabi**
Email: **rahman@alkaabi.co.em**
Phone number: **019 234 7921**

2	**UNIVERSITY OF CAMBRIDGE**

STUDENT ID CARD

First name: **Sheikha**
Family name: **Al Shahrani**
Email: **sheikha@alshahrani.co.sa**
Phone number: **04875 267 930**

---

1 His first name is

3 His phone number is

5 Her email address is

☐ 019 234 7921.

1 Ahmad.

☐ rahman@alkaabi.co.em.

2 His email address is

4 Her first name is

6 Her phone number is

☐ 04875 267 930.

☐ sheikha@alshahrani.co.sa.

☐ Sheikha.

6 🔊 **1.12** Read and listen. Match. Then trace.

1 ☐

a

☐ ☐

b

1 Her first name is Fatima.

2 His first name is Badir.

3 Her family name is Al Kamal.

4 His family name is Al Zaabi.

NOTICE ❗

→ his 👤 His name is Ahmad.

→ her 👤 Her name is Sheikha.

7 Read and circle.

1 **his**	→ has	→ hi	→ (his)	→ hiss	→ (his)
2 **her**	→ hero	→ her	→ here	→ hire	→ her
3 **number**	→ name	→ number	→ number	→ nobody	→ nimble
4 **first**	→ first	→ frost	→ fist	→ first	→ fast

8 Cover and complete.

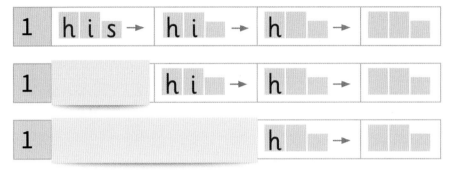

9 Continue.

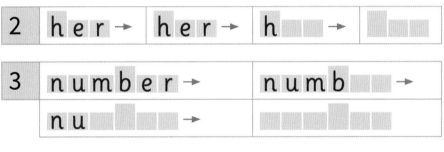

10 🔊 1.13 Writing Challenge Read and write. Then listen and check.

His   Her   number   first

1   His __ __ __ __ __ name is Salim.

2   __ __ __ family name is Al Hazmi.

3   __ __ __ name is Sara Al Qubtan.

4   Her phone __ __ __ __ __ __ is 04855 389 910.

1 🔊 **1.14** Write the countries. Then listen.

→ Mexico   India   Saudi Arabia   Turkey
→ Japan   the UK   Bahrain   Portugal

NOTICE ❗

Turkey   Saudi   Arabia

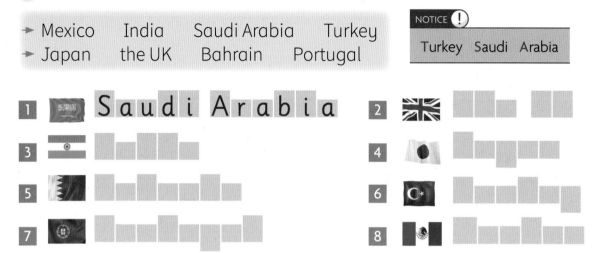

1 — S a u d i   A r a b i a

2 —

3 —

4 —

5 —

6 —

7 —

8 —

2 🔊 **1.15** Listen and say.

•• •	•• •	•••	•• •
Japan Bahrain	Turkey	India Mexico Portugal	the UK

3 🔊 **1.16** Where are they from? Listen, read and match.

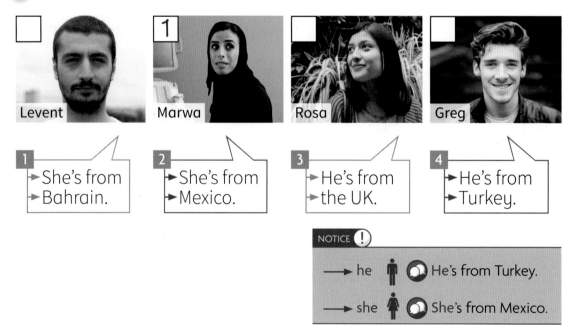

Levent   Marwa **1**   Rosa   Greg

1 → She's from → Bahrain.

2 → She's from → Mexico.

3 → He's from → the UK.

4 → He's from → Turkey.

NOTICE ❗

→ he 🧍 🌗 He's from Turkey.

→ she 🧍 🌗 She's from Mexico.

4 🔊 1.17 Read and (circle). Listen and check. Then trace.

1 (She is)/ He is from Japan.

2 She is / He is from Portugal.

3 She is / He is from India.

4 She is / He is from Saudi Arabia.

5 🔊 1.18 Listen, read and match. Then say.

| 2 | | |

a

b

1 She is from the UK.   2 He is from Mexico.

3 He is a student.   4 She is a teacher.

5 His name is Pedro.   6 Her name is Mrs Baker.

6 Writing Challenge Write about your teacher.

He is from Saudi Arabia.

SOUND AND SPELLING *p, b*

7 🔊 **1.19** Listen and read. Then trace.

→ Bb a bus to Bahrain

→ Pp palm trees in Portugal

8 🔊 **1.20** Look and listen. Then say.

Pp			
push		**p**ack	
pea		**p**ear	
pill		**p**in	

Bb			
bush		**b**ack	
bee		**b**ear	
bill		**b**in	

9 🔊 **1.21** Listen and draw.

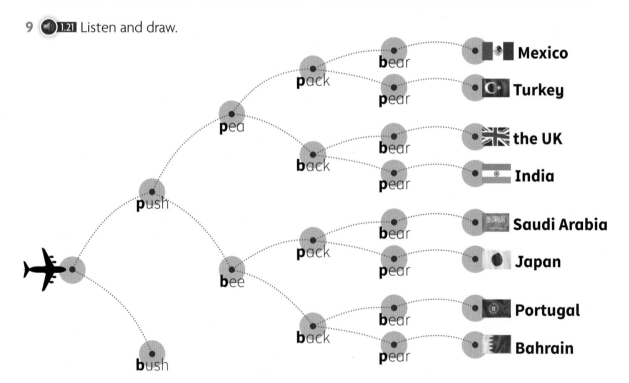

Where is the plane going? _____

LANGUAGE FOCUS

1 🔊 1.22 Listen and read. Trace. Then write.

library card

library card

student ID card

pen

pencil

book

notebook

mobile phone

dictionary

2 🔊 1.23 Read and (circle). Listen and check.

1 Can I have **a library card** / **a mobile phone**, please?

2 Can I have **a library card** / **a student ID card**, please?

3 Can I have **a book** / **a pen**, please?

4 Can I have **a pencil** / **a pen**, please?

3 🔊 1.24 Listen. Then trace. Listen again and say.

Bb   book   notebook   mobile

Pp   pen   pencil   please

4 Write.

What's the word in the box? _____

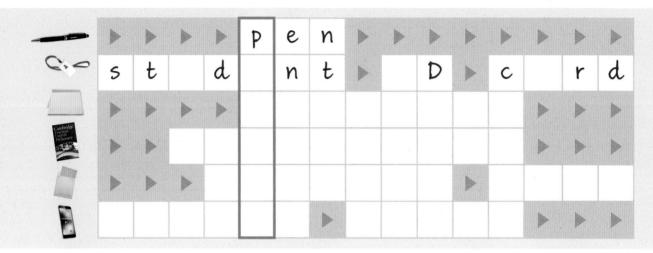

5 🔊 **1.25** Listen and read. Then listen and say.

1

▶ Can I have a book, please?

▶ Here you are.

2

▶ Can I have a pen, please?

▶ No, sorry.

6 Read and correct.

1 Can I have a ~~bencil~~, please? → **pencil** _____

2 Can I have a ~~notepook~~, please? → _____

3 Can I have a ~~bictionary~~, please? → _____

4 Can I have a ~~pook~~, please? → _____

5 Can I have a library card, ~~blease~~? → _____

SOUND AND SPELLING Short vowels

7 🔊 1.26 Listen and read. Then trace.

→ **Aa** Can I have a salad?

→ **Ee** There are ten lemons.

→ **Ii** His name is Tim.

→ **Oo** The doctor needs coffee.

→ **Uu** Run for the bus!

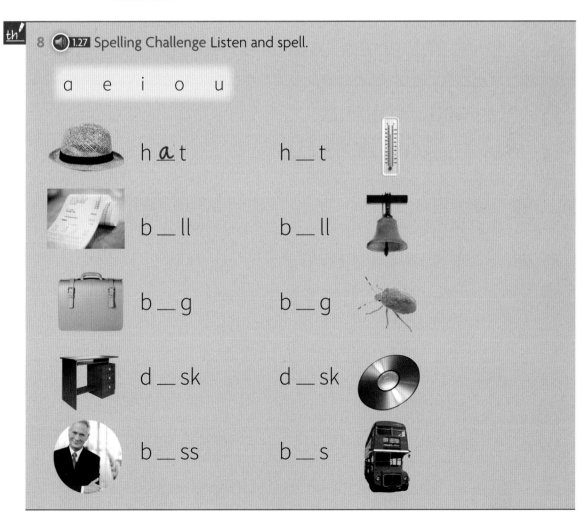

8 🔊 1.27 Spelling Challenge Listen and spell.

a   e   i   o   u

h **a** t   h __ t

b __ ll   b __ ll

b __ g   b __ g

d __ sk   d __ sk

b __ ss   b __ s

1 🔊 **1.28** Listen and look.

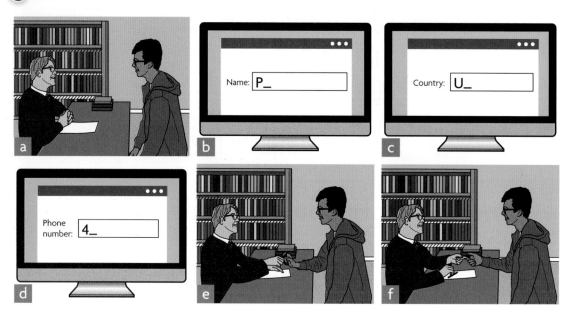

2 🔊 **1.29** Listen and (circle).

1 He needs a (**library card**)/ **student ID card**.

2 His first name is **Badir** / **Paddy**.

3 He's from **the UK** / **the UAE**.

4 His number is **443 218** / **453 218**.

5 He needs a **pencil** / **pen**.

3 Look at **1**. Read and match.

1 What's your phone number? $\boxed{d}$

2 Can I have a pen, please? $\boxed{}$

3 Where are you from? $\boxed{}$

4 Can I have a library card, please? $\boxed{}$

5 What's your first name? $\boxed{}$

4 🔊 **1.30** Find the words. Then listen and check.

1 Can|I|have|a|library|card,|please?

2 Whereareyoufrom?

3 What'syourname?

4 CanIhaveapen?

⊙ KEY WORDS FOR LITERACY

1 🔊 **1.31** Listen, read and ⬭circle⬭.

1 **he** Where is ⬭he⬭ from? ⬭He⬭'s from Bahrain.

2 **she** She's from India. She's a teacher.

3 **you** Where are you from?

4 **the** He's from the UK. She's from the UAE.

2 Read and ⬭circle⬭.

1 **he**	→	her	→	hi	→	he	→	here	→	he
2 **she**	→	she	→	he's	→	shed	→	she	→	he
3 **you**	→	your	→	you	→	young	→	you	→	yours
4 **the**	→	the	→	there	→	the	→	he	→	them

3 Cover and complete.

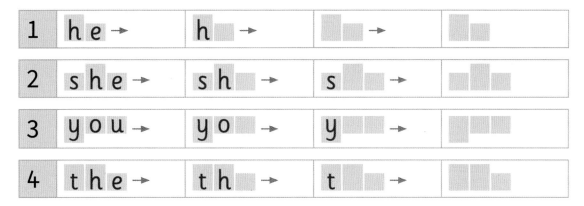

1	h e →	h →	→	
2	s h e →	s h →	s →	
3	y o u →	y o →	y →	
4	t h e →	t h →	t →	

4 🔊 **1.32** Read and write. Then listen and check.

1 Where are **y o u** from?   **2** I am from ▯▯▯ UK.

3 ▯ is from Mexico.   **4** ▯▯ is a teacher.

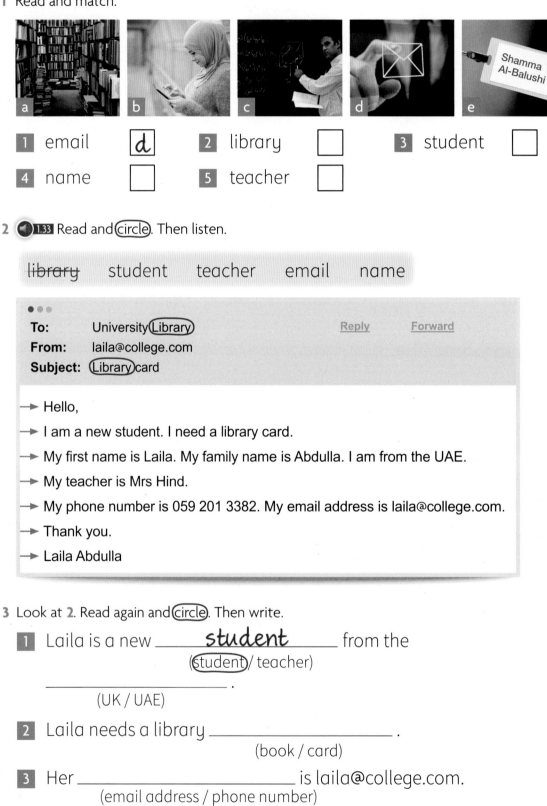

1 Read and match.

a · b · c · d · e

1 email — *d* 2 library — ☐ 3 student — ☐

4 name — ☐ 5 teacher — ☐

2 🔊 1.33 Read and (circle). Then listen.

~~library~~   student   teacher   email   name

To: University (Library)   *Reply*   *Forward*
From: laila@college.com
Subject: (Library) card

→ Hello,

→ I am a new student. I need a library card.

→ My first name is Laila. My family name is Abdulla. I am from the UAE.

→ My teacher is Mrs Hind.

→ My phone number is 059 201 3382. My email address is laila@college.com.

→ Thank you.

→ Laila Abdulla

3 Look at 2. Read again and (circle). Then write.

1 Laila is a new _____**student**_____ from the
    ((student) / teacher)

    _____ .
    (UK / UAE)

2 Laila needs a library _____ .
    (book / card)

3 Her _____ is laila@college.com.
    (email address / phone number)

4 Read. Then write with CAPITAL letters.

~~omar~~   oman   khalid

UNIVERSITY OF CAMBRIDGE

First name: _____ *Omar* _____

Family name: _____

Country: _____

Phone number: **043 78 3 4323**

Email: **omar1999@edu.com**

5 🔊 **1.34** Find the words. Then listen and check.

1 My|name|isOmarKhalid.

2 IamfromOman.

3 Iamastudent.

4 Myphonenumberis0437834323.

5 Myemailaddressisomar1999@edu.com.

6 Read and correct.

1 ~~my~~ name is Omar Khalid.   → My _____

2 I am from ~~oman~~.   → _____

3 ~~I~~am a student.   → _____

4 My phone ~~Number~~ is 0437834323.   → _____

7 Write about you.

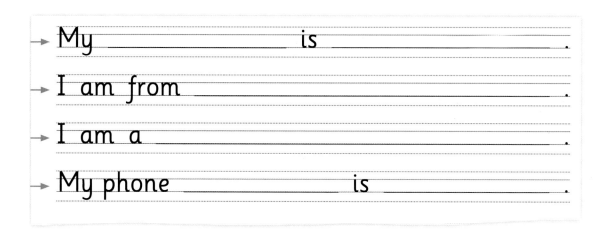

→ My _____ is _____.

→ I am from _____.

→ I am a _____.

→ My phone _____ is _____.

UNIT 2 PEOPLE AND THINGS

LISTENING AND READING 1

1 🔊 **2.1** Listen and read. Then trace. Listen again and say.

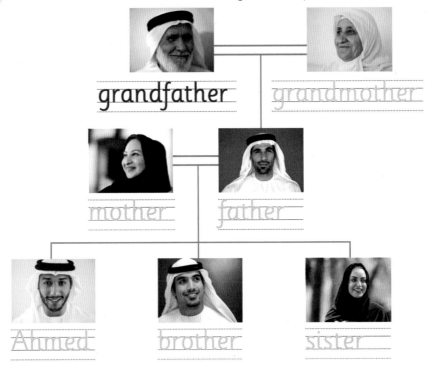

grandfather   grandmother

mother   father

Ahmed   brother   sister

2 🔊 **2.2** Read and write. Then listen.

grandmother   mother   brother   grandfather   ~~sister~~   father

1 This is my **s i s t e r** .

2 This is my ⬚⬚⬚⬚⬚⬚ .

3 This is my ⬚⬚⬚⬚⬚⬚⬚ .

4 This is my ⬚⬚⬚⬚⬚⬚ .

5 This is my ⬚⬚⬚⬚⬚⬚⬚⬚⬚⬚⬚ .

6 This is my ⬚⬚⬚⬚⬚⬚⬚⬚⬚⬚⬚ .

SOUND AND SPELLING *th*

3 🔊 **2.3** Listen and read. Then trace. Listen again and say.

→ mo th er   grandfa th er

4 🔊 **2.4** Listen and read. Then write. Listen again and say.

→ bro____er   grandmo____er   fa____er

5 🔊 **2.5** Look and match. Then listen and check.

a	b	c	d
Ali Hussain	Sally Jacks	Maya Allen	Yousif Suleman

1 Dr Allen

3 Dr Suleman

2 Mr Hussain

4 Mrs Jacks

6 Read and circle.

1 **Mrs** → Mr → (Mrs) → Mr → Dr → Mrs → Mr → Mrs → Dr

2 **Mr** → Dr → Mr → Dr → Mrs → Mr → Mr → Mrs → Mr

3 **Dr** → Mr → Mrs → Mr → Dr → Dr → Mr → Mrs → Dr

NOTICE ❗

→ Maya Allen is a doctor.

→ Her name is Dr Allen.   ~~Dr Maya~~

7 🔊 **2.6** Read and (circle). Then listen and check.

→ This is my teacher. His name
→ is **Mr Berry** / **Mrs Berry**.

→ This is my doctor. Her name
→ is **Dr Sue** / **Dr Davey**.

→ This is my teacher. Her name
→ is **Mrs Jan** / **Mrs Spring**.

→ This is my father. His name
→ is **Mr Rashid** / **Mrs Rashid**.

8 Read. Write ▪ and the CAPITAL letters.

1 ~~t~~T̲his is my father **.**

2 This is my teacher

3 Her name is Maya allen **.**

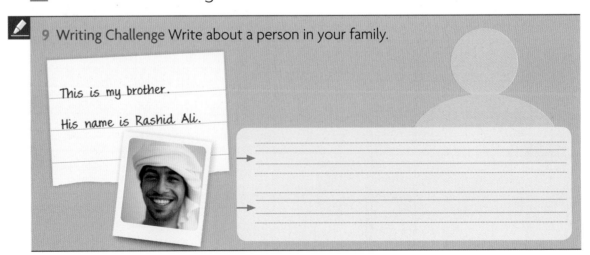

✏️ **9** Writing Challenge Write about a person in your family.

This is my brother.

His name is Rashid Ali.

LISTENING AND READING 2

1 🔊 2.7 Listen and read. Then trace. Say.

→ Hi! I'm Saeed.

→ I'm from Oman.

→ We're sisters.

→ We're from Mexico.

→ They're brothers.

→ They're from the UK.

→ She's a teacher.

→ She's from Turkey.

2 🔊 2.8 Listen and underline. Then trace.

→ I am / They are Lana and this is Tala.

→ I am / We are sisters.

→ I am / We are brothers.

→ I am / We are from Turkey.

→ This is / They are Mrs Antaki and this

→ is Mr Lodge. I am / They are teachers.

NOTICE ❗

→ I am a student. → He is a teacher.

→ We are students. → They are teachers.

3 🔊 **2.9** Read and write. Then listen.

I am a student.

I'm a student.

NOTICE ❗

🔊 ✏️

→ I'm = I am
→ He's = He is
→ She's = She is
→ We're = We are
→ They're = They are

She is a doctor.

▢▢▢▢▢ a doctor.

He is from the UK.

▢▢▢▢ from the UK.

We are brothers.

▢▢▢▢ brothers.

They are teachers.

▢▢▢▢▢▢ teachers.

4 🔊 **2.10** Find the words. Then listen and say.

1 We|are|students.

2 They'refromJapan.

3 I'mfromtheUAE.

4 She'sateacher.

5 We'refromSaudiArabia.

6 Theyarestudents.

5 Read and circle.

My   his   Our   Their

→ We're from Qatar.
→ My name is Suhail
  and his name is Sami.
→ Our teachers are from the UK.
→ Their names are Mr Little
  and Mr Marley.

NOTICE ⚠

→ We are students.
Our names are Jon and Sam.

→ They are teachers.
Their names are Mr Ali and
Mr Timms.

6 Read and circle. Then correct.

1 → We aer from the UAE. _are_

2 → I aem from Oman. _____

3 → Oure teachers are from the UK. _____

4 → Thier names are Ali and Obaid. _____

5 → He is a taecher. _____

6 → She is a studant. _____

7 Writing Challenge Write about two teachers.

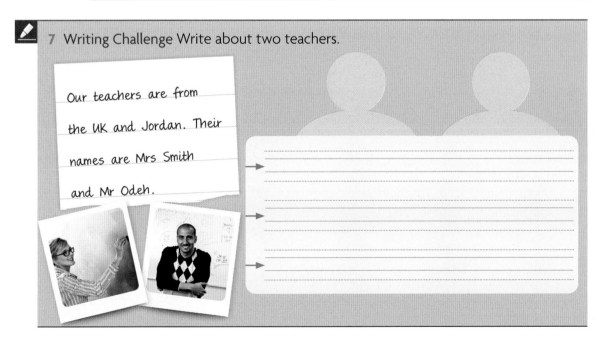

Our teachers are from
the UK and Jordan. Their
names are Mrs Smith
and Mr Odeh.

LISTENING AND READING 3

1 🔊 **2.11** Write. Then listen.

9	3	7	8	5	4	6

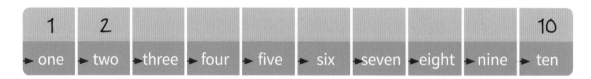

1	2								10
▸ one	▸ two	▸ three	▸ four	▸ five	▸ six	▸ seven	▸ eight	▸ nine	▸ ten

2 🔊 **2.12** How many? Write the number. Then listen.

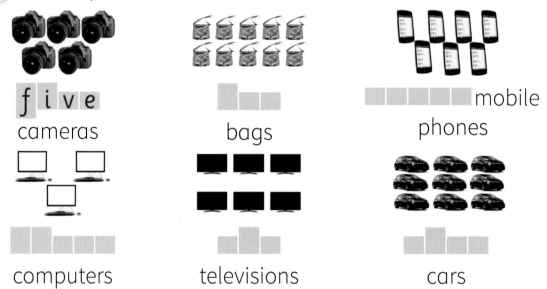

f i v e
cameras

bags

mobile phones

computers

televisions

cars

3 🔊 **2.13** Find the words. Then listen and check.

one|two|foureightoneeightfourtwofouroneeighttwooneeighttwofour

4 Cover and complete.

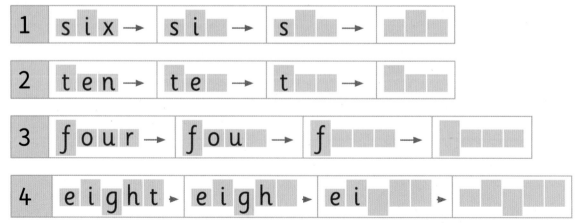

1 s i x → s i ▢ → s ▢▢ → ▢▢▢

2 t e n → t e ▢ → t ▢▢ → ▢▢▢

3 f o u r → f o u ▢ → f ▢▢▢ → ▢▢▢▢

4 e i g h t ▸ e i g h ▸ e i ▢▢▢ ▸ ▢▢▢▢▢

5 🔊 2.14 Listen and read. Then trace. Listen again and say.

1 → How many cars do you have?

2 → How many televisions do you have?

3 → How many computers do you have?

4 → How many bags do you have?

NOTICE ⚠
→ one car
→ two cameras
→ six bags

6 Read and circle. Correct.

I have one cars. → car

I have two bag. → _____

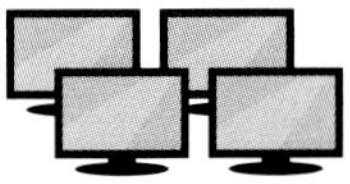

We have four television. → _____

We have one computers. → _____

7 Write the sentences.

1 three / computers. / have / We

→ We have three computers.

2 have / We / two / televisions.

→ _____

3 bags. / have / four / I

→ _____

4 seven / I / have / mobile phones.

→ _____

SOUND AND SPELLING Word stress

8 🔊 **2.15** Look and listen. Then say.

● ●
seven

● ● ●
Mexico

9 🔊 **2.16** Look and listen. Match and write **1**, **2** or **3**. Then listen and check.

1 ● ●   　　　**2** ● ● ●　　　**3** ● ● ● ●

teacher	1	grandmother	2
doctor	1	television	
Mexico		sister	
family		grandfather	
brother		father	
mother		student	

10 🔊 **2.17** Match and ⬭circle. Then listen and check.

1 ● ● ●	(family)	sister	(grandmother)
2 ● ●	brother	Mexico	Turkey
3 ● ● ●	father	grandfather	family
4 ● ●	student	doctor	grandmother

LANGUAGE FOCUS

1 ◀ 2.18 Look and listen. Then write.

11   eleven   • • • • • • • • • • • •

12   twelve   • • • • • • • • • • • • •

1__   thirteen   • • • • • • • • • • • • •

14   ___four_teen   • • • • • • • • • • • • • •

1__   fifteen   • • • • • • • • • • • • • • •

16   _____teen   • • • • • • • • • • • • • • • •

17   _____teen   • • • • • • • • • • • • • • • • •

__ __   eighteen   • • • • • • • • • • • • • • • • • •

19   _____teen   • • • • • • • • • • • • • • • • • • •

2 ◀ 2.19 Look and find the words. Then listen and check.

| 17 | 11 | 13 | 19 | 12 | 18 | 14 | 16 | 15 |

seventeen|eleventhirteennineteentwelveeighteenfourteensixteenfifteen

3 ◀ 2.20 Write. Listen. Then trace.

| 40 | ~~20~~ | 60 | 100 | ~~30~~ | 80 | 90 | 50 | 70 |

20	→ **twenty**	30	→ thirty	☐	→ forty
☐	→ fifty	☐	→ sixty	☐	→ seventy
☐	→ eighty	☐	→ ninety	☐	→ **one** hundred

4 🔊 **2.21** Read and circle. Listen and check. Then trace.

→ 14 fourteen / forty   → 70 seventeen / seventy

→ 50 fifteen / fifty   → 16 sixteen / sixty

→ 30 thirteen / thirty   → 19 nineteen / ninety

5 🔊 **2.22** Read and write. Then listen and check.

→ This is Osama.   20 He is _____twenty_____ years old.

→ This is Dr Taleb.   40 He is _____ years old.

→ This is Omar.   12 He is _____ years old.

→ This is Mrs Hussain. 80 She is _____ years old.

→ This is Fatima.   8 She is _____ years old.

✏️ **6** Writing Challenge Write about your family.

This is Majid, my brother. He is twenty years old.

→ _____, my _____

→ _____ is _____ years old.

SOUND AND SPELLING Silent *e* – *name, nine* ...

7 🔊 **2.23** Listen and read. Then trace. Listen again and say.

→ plane → hate → cake → name → shave

8 🔊 **2.24** Listen and read. Then trace. Listen again and say.

→ nine → kite → rice → pine → lime

9 🔊 **2.25** Listen and read.

1 plan plane
2 hat hate
3 can cane
4 pin pine

10 🔊 **2.26** Look at **9**. Listen and circle.

11 🔊 **2.27** Spelling Challenge Listen and write. Then listen and check.

1 d _ t _   2 l _ m _   3 c _ p _   4 p _ p _

1 🔊 **2.28** Read and match. Then listen and check.

→ My bag
→ Country: Turkey
→ Years: 2

a

→ My car
→ Country: Japan
→ Years: 3

b

1	This is my car.	b	**2**	My bag is from Turkey.	☐
3	This is my bag.	☐	**4**	My car is from Japan.	☐
5	My bag is two years old.	☐	**6**	My car is three years old.	☐

2 🔊 **2.29** Find the words. Listen and say. Then match.

1	This|is|mygrandfather.	b	**2**	Heis41yearsold.	a
3	HeisfromOman.	☐	**4**	Thisismyteacher.	☐
5	Heis79yearsold.	☐	**6**	HeisfromtheUK.	☐

⊙ KEY WORDS FOR LITERACY

1 🔊 **2.30** Read and ⟨circle⟩. Then listen.

1	**are**	They ⟨are⟩ from the UK.	**2**	**is**	My car is from Japan.
3	**one**	I have one bag.	**4**	**two**	She is two years old.
5	**from**	He is from the UK.			

2 Read and ⟨circle⟩.

1	**are**	→	⟨are⟩	→	our	→	am	→	are	→	are
2	**is**	→	is	→	in	→	as	→	is	→	in
3	**one**	→	on	→	one	→	one	→	in	→	on
4	**two**	→	to	→	too	→	two	→	to	→	two
5	**from**	→	from	→	room	→	from	→	farm	→	from

3 Cover and complete.

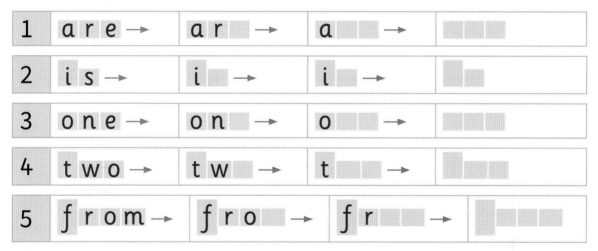

1 a r e → a r ☐ → a ☐ ☐ → ☐ ☐ ☐

2 i s → i ☐ → i ☐ → ☐ ☐

3 o n e → o n ☐ → o ☐ ☐ → ☐ ☐ ☐

4 t w o → t w ☐ → t ☐ ☐ → ☐ ☐ ☐

5 f r o m → f r o ☐ → f r ☐ ☐ → ☐ ☐ ☐ ☐

4 🔊 **2.31** Read and write. Then listen and check.

1 We **a r e** from Oman.

2 Their television is ＿ ＿ ＿ ＿ Japan.

3 We have ＿ ＿ ＿ computer.

4 He ＿ ＿ seventeen years old.

5 My mobile phone is ＿ ＿ ＿ years old.

READING AND WRITING

1 Look and match.

I'm Alia.

a

b

c

d

e

1 our teacher ☐ c   **2** our class ☐   **3** dictionaries ☐

4 friends ☐   **5** computers ☐

2 🔊 **2.32** Look at **1**. Read and circle. Then listen.

→ This is our class. We have thirty dictionaries. We have six computers.
→ Our teacher is from the UK. Her name is Mrs Randall. She is forty
→ years old. Carlos is from Mexico. He is nineteen. Riku and Taro are
→ friends. They are from Japan. Riku is twenty-two years old. Taro is
→ twenty-three years old.

3 Look at **2**. Read again and match.

1 **We** have 30 dictionaries.   Carlos

2 **She** is 40 years old.   Our class

3 **He** is 19.   Riku and Taro

4 **They** are from Japan.   Mrs Randall

4 Look and correct.

1 i　f r e n d　→ _friend_

2 a　t e c h e r　→ _____

3 e　s t u d n t　→ _____

4 a　c l s s　→ _____

5 e　c o m p u t r　→ _____

5 Read and correct.

1 our　　This is^*our* class.　→ _our_

2 have　　We 10 computers.　→ _____

3 is　　His name Jack.　→ _____

4 from　　She is the UK.　→ _____

5 my　　He is friend.　→ _____

6 Write about your class.

→ This is our class.

→ We have _____ computers.

→ This is my teacher.

→ _____ name is _____.

→ This is _____.

→ _____ is my friend.

→ _____ is from _____.

UNIT 3 UNIVERSITY LIFE

LISTENING AND READING 1

1 🔊 **3.1** Look and match. Then listen.

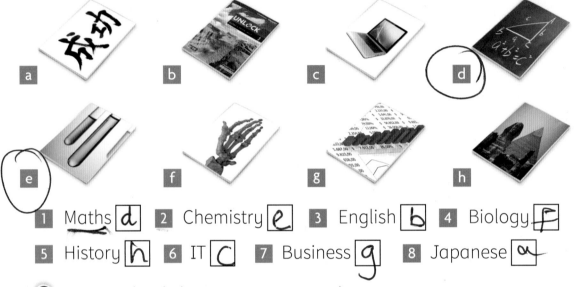

a   b   c   d (circled)

e (circled)   f   g   h

1 Maths $\boxed{d}$ **2** Chemistry $\boxed{e}$ **3** English $\boxed{b}$ **4** Biology $\boxed{f}$

5 History $\boxed{h}$ **6** IT $\boxed{c}$ **7** Business $\boxed{g}$ **8** Japanese $\boxed{a}$

2 🔊 **3.2** Listen and read. Then trace. Listen again and say.

1 Maths   **2** Chemistry   **3** English

4 Biology   **5** History   **6** IT

7 Business   **8** Japanese

3 🔊 **3.3** Listen again and complete.

1 Maths   **2** Chemistry

3 English   **4** Biology

5 History   **6** IT

7 Business   **8** Japanese

4 🔊 **3.4** Look at **1**. Say and write. Then listen and check.

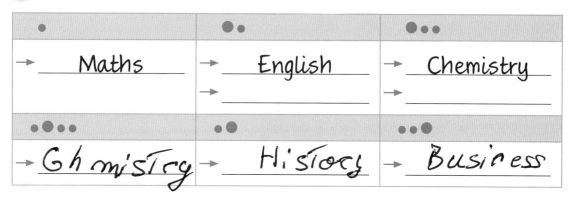

•	••	•••
→ Maths	→ English	→ Chemistry
	→ _____	→ _____

•••••	••	•••
→ Ghmistry	→ History	→ Business

5 🔊 **3.5** Read and match. Then listen and check.

NOTICE ❗
⟶ I study English, Japanese and History.

1 → What subjects → do you study?

2 → What subjects → do you study?

→ I study Chemistry, → Biology and Maths.

→ I study English, → Japanese and History.

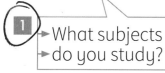

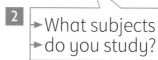

2   a   1   b   1   c   2   d   2   e   1   f

6 🔊 **3.6** Trace and write. Then listen and check.

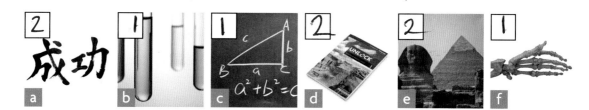

English   Maths   Chemistry   Biology   Business   Japanese

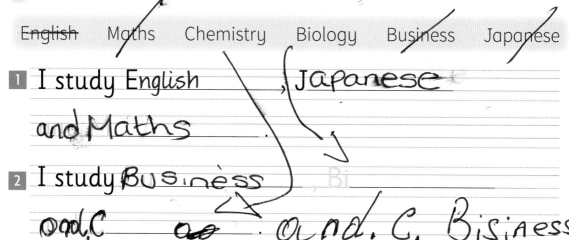

1 I study English , Japanese and Maths .

2 I study Business and C ao . and. C. Bisiaess

7 Read and write **,** , **.** and **?** .

  1 I study Maths__English and Biology__

  2 I study History__Chemistry and IT__

  3 I study Business__Maths and Japanese__

  4 What subjects do you study__

8 🔊 **3.7** Find the words. Then listen and check.

  1 I|study|Japanese,BusinessandIT.

  2 IstudyIT,EnglishandHistory.

  3 IstudyChemistry,BiologyandMaths.

  4 Whatsubjectsdoyoustudy?

9 🔊 **3.8** Listen and write.

  1 M_aths_____   **2** C_____

  3 E_____   **4** B_____

  5 H_____   **6** I_____

  7 B_____   **8** J_____

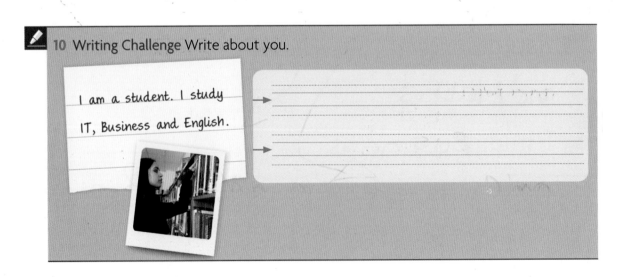

10 Writing Challenge Write about you.

I am a student. I study
IT, Business and English.

LISTENING AND READING 2

1 🔊 **3.9** Match. Then listen and check.

SU	M	TU	W	TH	F	SA
1	2	3	4	5	6	7

Friday ☐   Monday ☐   Sunday ☐ 1   Wednesday ☐

Tuesday ☐   Thursday ☐   Saturday ☐

2 🔊 **3.10** Trace. Then listen and say.

Sunday   Monday   Tuesday   Wednesday

Thursday   Friday   Saturday

> **NOTICE** ⓘ
>
> ~~monday~~
>
> Monday Tuesday Wednesday

3 🔊 **3.11** Read and ⬭circle. Then listen and check.

1	**Sunday** → Saturday → ⬭Sunday → Saturday → Sunday
2	**Thursday** → Thursday → Tuesday → Tuesday → Thursday
3	**Saturday** → Saturday → Sunday → Saturday → Sunday
4	**Tuesday** → Tuesday → Thursday → Thursday → Tuesday

4 Look and complete.

1 M☐☐☐☐☐☐   2 F☐☐☐☐☐   3 Tu☐☐☐☐☐

4 Su☐☐☐☐   5 Th☐☐☐☐☐☐

6 W☐☐☐☐☐☐☐☐   7 Sa☐☐☐☐☐

5 🔊 **3.12** Listen and read. Then match and trace. Listen again and say.

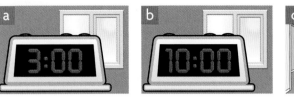

1	**morning**	b
2	afternoon	☐
3	room	☐
4	class	☐

6 🔊 **3.13** Read and match. Then listen and check.

1 Where is our English class?   In room 3.

2 When is our IT class?   On Monday morning.

3 Where is our Maths class?   In room 7.

4 When is our Business class?   On Tuesday afternoon.

	Sunday	**Monday**	**Tuesday**
Morning	Maths	Business	History
	room 3	room 14	room 6
Afternoon	English	Biology	IT
	room 7	room 20	room 16

7 Read and write *In* or *On*.

1 Where is our Business class? __In__ room 12.   Yes (No)

2 When is our History class?   ____ Tuesday.   Yes No

3 When is our Biology class?   ____ Sunday.   Yes No

4 Where is our English class? ____ room 7.   Yes No

8 Look at **6** and **7**. (Circle) *Yes* or *No*.

NOTICE ❗
→ On Monday afternoon.
→ In room 7.

9 🔊 3.14 Read and circle. Then listen.

1 **afternoon** I study Chemistry on Friday afternoon.

2 **study**   I study Maths in room 8.

3 **morning**   I study History on Tuesday morning.

10 Read and circle.

1 **afternoon**	→	after nine	→	afternoon	→	afternoon
2 **study**	→	stop	→	sturdy	→	study
3 **morning**	→	mourning	→	moaning	→	morning

11 Cover and complete.

1 a f t e r n o o n → a f t e r n _ _ _ →
a f t _ _ _ _ _ →

2 s t u d y → s t u _ → s t _ _ → _ _ _ _

3 m o r n i n g → m o r _ _ _ →
m o _ _ _ →

12 Read and circle. Correct.

1 I study (maths) on (monday) morning.

<u>I study Maths on Monday morning.</u>

2 I study business on wednesday afternoon.

_____

3 I study english on tuesday morning.

_____

1 🔊 **3.15** Listen and read. Then trace. Listen again and say.

interesting

boring

easy

difficult

2 🔊 **3.16** Listen, read and match.

1 ●● **2** ●●●

boring 1   interesting ☐   easy ☐   difficult ☐

3 🔊 **3.17** Listen and read. Then listen and match.

1 ➤ What's Maths like?

➤ It's easy. It isn't difficult.

2 ➤ What's IT like?

➤ It's boring. It isn't ➤ interesting.

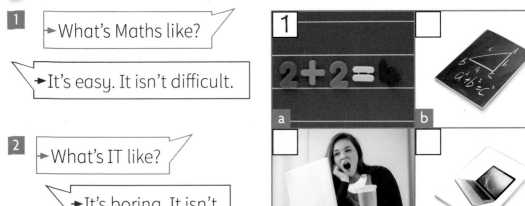

NOTICE ❗

💬 It's easy. ➜ ✏️ It is easy.
It isn't boring. ➜ It is not boring.

4 Write.

1 ➤ It isn't difficult.

It __is__ __not__ difficult.

2 ➤ It's easy.

It _____ easy.

3 ➤ It isn't boring.

It _____ _____ boring.

4 ➤ What's it like?

What _____ it like?

5 🔊 **3.18** Read and (circle). Listen and check. Then trace.

1 It is easy. ~~It is~~ / (It is not) difficult.

2 It is interesting. It is / It is not boring.

3 It is not easy. It is / It is not difficult.

4 It is not interesting. It is / It is not boring.

6 Read and (circle). Correct.

1 It is (diffcult). → It is difficult.

2 It is not eesy. → _____

3 It is intersting. → _____

4 It is not baring. → _____

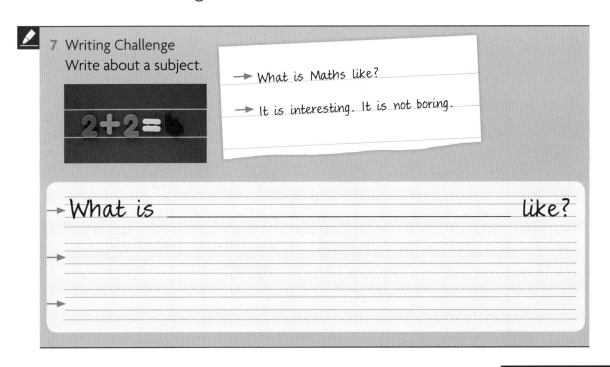

7 Writing Challenge
Write about a subject.

→ What is Maths like?

→ It is interesting. It is not boring.

→ What is _____ like?

SOUND AND SPELLING *sh*, *ch*, *th*

8 🔊 **3.19** Listen and read. Then trace. Listen again and say.

How many English teachers do you have?

I have three English teachers.

9 🔊 **3.20** Listen and read. Then trace. Listen again and say.

shop cheese thin

shoe cherry thick

wash peach tooth

brush lunch mouth

fish bench bath

10 🔊 **3.21** Listen and read.

 1 ship chip   **2** chin thin

 3 thin shin   **4** teach teeth

11 🔊 **3.22** Look at **10**. Listen and (circle).

LANGUAGE FOCUS

1 Look. Then match and write.

one　~~two~~　eight　four

1 ____two____ o'clock　　**2** _____ o'clock

3 _____-thirty　　**4** _____-thirty

2 🔊 **3.23** Read and listen. Then match and trace. Listen again and say.

1

2

3

4

It is three-thirty.

It is five o'clock.

It is seven o'clock.

It is nine-thirty.

3 🔊 **3.24** Look and write. Then listen and check.

1 It is s _i_ x-_t_ _h_ _i_ _r_ _t_ _y_ .

2 It is __ w ____ __ __ __'c ___ __ k.

3 It is ___ __'_____.

4 It is _____-_____.

4 🔊 **3.25** Read and match. Then listen and check.

| Tuesday | 10:00 | IT | 3:30 | Maths |

1 ➤When is our IT class?

2 ➤What time is our IT class?

3 ➤When is our Maths class?

4 ➤What time is our Maths class?

➤On Tuesday afternoon.

➤ It's at three-thirty.

➤It's at ten o'clock.

➤On Tuesday morning.

5 Read and ⟨circle⟩. Correct.

1 It is at three ⟨clock⟩. → *It is at three o'clock.*

2 It is thirty-twelve. → _____

3 It is five o'clocks. → _____

6 🔊 **3.26** Read and write. Then listen and check.

1 What time is our Business class?

It is at _____ .

2 What time is our English class?

It is _____ .

3 What time is our IT class?
It _____ .

4 What time is our Biology class?

_____ .

📱 9:47 AM

WEDNESDAY

9:00	English
12:30	IT
2:00	Business
3:00	Biology

SOUND AND SPELLING Silent *e* – *ph***o***ne, c***u***te* ...

7 🔊 **3.27** Listen and read. Then trace. Listen again and say.

phone   b**o**ne   c**o**d**e**   r**o**p**e**

8 🔊 **3.28** Listen and read. Then trace. Listen again and say.

computer   c**u**t**e**   t**u**b**e**   d**u**n**e**

9 🔊 **3.29** Listen and read.

 1 cod code

 2 rob robe

 3 not note

4 cut cute

10 🔊 **3.30** Look at **9**. Listen and (circle).

th **11** 🔊 **3.31** Spelling Challenge Listen and write. Then listen and check.

1 h **o** m **e**

2 st __ d __ nt

3 perf __ m __

4 h __ l __

5 gl __ b __

6 d __ n __

1 🔊 **3.32** Read and listen. Complete. Then listen and check.

interesting ~~History~~ boring English
Business easy difficult

1 H i s t o r y **2** ▢▢▢▢▢▢▢▢▢▢

3 ▢▢▢▢▢ **4** ▢▢▢▢▢

5 ▢▢▢▢▢▢ **6** ▢▢▢▢▢▢▢ **7** ▢▢▢▢

2 🔊 **3.33** Listen and read. Then <u>underline</u>.

►What subjects do you study?

►What is History like?

► What is Business like?

► Where is your English class?

►I study History, Business
►and English.

►It's interesting.
►It's not boring.

►It's difficult.
►It's not easy.

►In room 10.

1 It is interesting. Business / History
2 It is not easy. English / Business
3 In room 10. English / History

NOTICE ❗

It's not = It isn't

3 Find the words.

1 What|subjects|doyoustudy? Business

2 Itisnotboring. room 10

3 Itisdifficult. History, Business and English

4 WhereisyourEnglishclass? History

4 🔊 **3.33** Look at **3**. Listen again and match.

⊙ KEY WORDS FOR LITERACY

1 🔊 3.34 Read and ⟨circle⟩. Then listen.

   1 it   ⟨It⟩ is in room 12.

   2 at   Our class is at two o'clock.

   3 in   I study Maths in room 8.

   4 on   I study History on Tuesday morning.

2 Read and ⟨circle⟩.

1 it	→	at	→	⟨it⟩	→	is	→	it	→	is
2 at	→	it	→	at	→	and	→	at	→	it
3 in	→	in	→	on	→	is	→	in	→	it
4 on	→	or	→	on	→	one	→	our	→	on

3 Cover and complete.

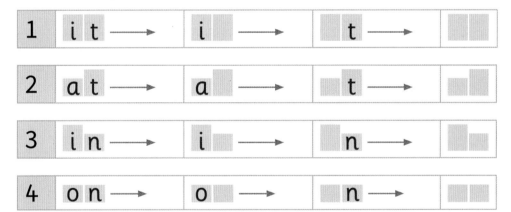

1 i t → i → t → ☐☐

2 a t → a → t → ☐☐

3 i n → i → n → ☐☐

4 o n → o → n → ☐☐

4 🔊 3.35 Read and write. Then listen and check.

   1 I study Maths _o_ _n_ Monday morning.

   2 It is __ __ seven o'clock.

   3 __ __ is on Wednesday morning.

   4 Our class is __ __ room 3.

READING AND WRITING

1 Look and write.

Days: Sunday [ ] o [ ] a [ ] ue [ ] a [ ]
[ ] e [ ] e [ ] a [ ] [ ] u [ ] a [ ]

Subjects: E [ ] i [ ] a [ ] [ ] e [ ] i [ ] [ ]
[ ] u [ ] i [ ] e [ ]

2 🔊 3.36 Look at 1. Read and (circle). Then listen.

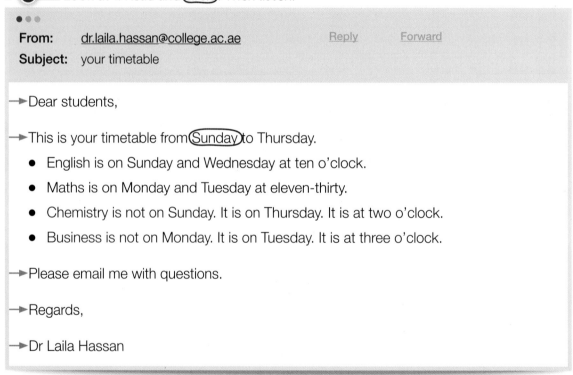

From: dr.laila.hassan@college.ac.ae   Reply   Forward
Subject: your timetable

→ Dear students,

→ This is your timetable from (Sunday) to Thursday.

- English is on Sunday and Wednesday at ten o'clock.
- Maths is on Monday and Tuesday at eleven-thirty.
- Chemistry is not on Sunday. It is on Thursday. It is at two o'clock.
- Business is not on Monday. It is on Tuesday. It is at three o'clock.

→ Please email me with questions.

→ Regards,

→ Dr Laila Hassan

3 Look at 2. Read again and complete.

	SUNDAY	MONDAY	TUESDAY	WEDNESDAY	THURSDAY
MORNING	English				
	————	11:30	11:30	10:00	
AFTERNOON			Business		
			————		2:00

4 Read and (circle). Correct.

1 Our Maths class is (at) Thursday morning.   _____on_____

2 Our english class is on Monday afternoon.   _____

3 It is in three-thirty.   _____

4 It is on wednesday afternoon.   _____

5 It is at tow o'clock.   _____

6 Our History class is on Tuesday afeternoon.   _____

5 Look. Then read and (circle).

THURSDAY
10:30
English
2:00
Maths

→ Our English class is on
   Thursday **morning** / **afternoon**.
→ It is at ten-thirty. Our Maths class
   is on Thursday **morning** / **afternoon**.
→ It is at two o'clock.

6 Complete your timetable and write.

_____ day

__ __ : __ __   _____

__ __ : __ __   _____

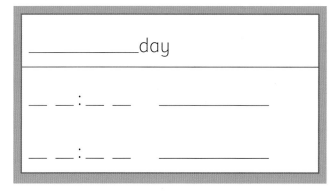

→ Our _____ class is on _____ morning.

→ It is at _____. Our _____ class is on

→ _____ afternoon. It is at _____.

UNIT 4 DIFFERENT COUNTRIES

LISTENING AND READING 1

1 🔊 4.1 Listen and read. Then trace. Listen again and say.

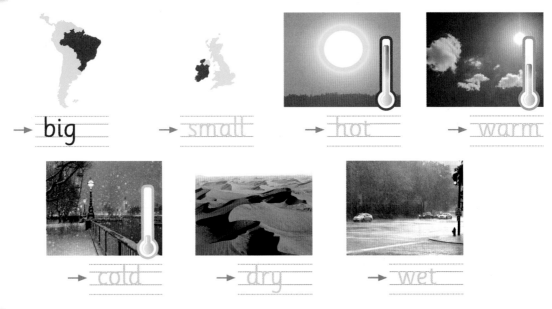

→ big → small → hot → warm

→ cold → dry → wet

2 🔊 4.2 Read and match. Then listen.

1	The UK is cold.	2	Greece is hot.
3	Saudi Arabia is dry.	4	Brazil is big.
5	France is warm.	6	Singapore is small and wet.

UNLOCK BASIC LITERACY

3 🔊 **4.3** Find the words. Then listen and check.

cold|smallhotwarmwetdrybig

4 Cover and complete.

1	w a r m → w a ☐ ☐	2	d r y ⟶ d ☐ ☐
3	w e t ⟶ w ☐ ☐	4	c o l d → c o ☐ ☐
5	h o t ⟶ h ☐ ☐	6	b i g ⟶ b ☐ ☐
7	s m a l l → s m a ☐ ☐		

5 Read, choose and write.

dry	big	small	cold	hot	~~wet~~	warm

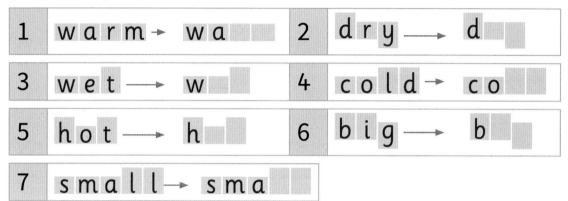

India   Canada

1 What is India like?
   It is ___wet___ .

2 What is Canada like?
   It is _____ .

Qatar   Russia

3 What is Qatar like?
   It is _____ .

4 What is Russia like?
   It is _____ .

6 🔊 4.4 Read and write. Then listen and check.

1 The UK is cold. The UK is wet.

The UK is ___*cold and wet*___ .

NOTICE ❗

Singapore is small.
Singapore is wet. =
Singapore is small
and wet.

2 France is big. France is warm.

France is _____ .

3 Canada is big. Canada is cold.

Canada _____ .

4 Saudi Arabia is dry. Saudi Arabia is hot.

_____ .

🖊 **7** Writing Challenge Write about your country.

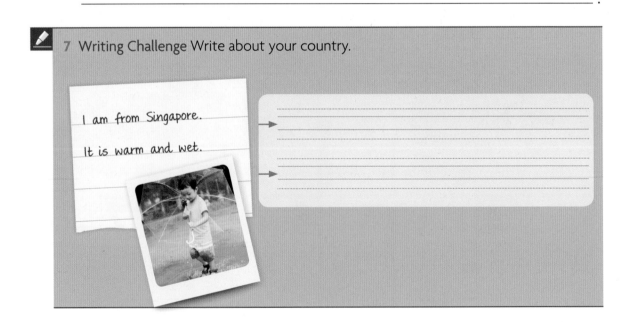

I am from Singapore.

It is warm and wet.

LISTENING AND READING 2

1 Read and match. Then trace.

1 It is in Turkey. — **c**

2 They are from Turkey. ☐

3 It is in the UK. ☐

4 They are from the UK. ☐

2 Read and circle.

1 in	→ is	→ (in)	→ it	→ in	→ on	
2 from	→ from	→ four	→ for	→ from	→ from	

3 🔊 4.5 Read and write. Then listen.

1 It is ▢ the UAE.   **2** They are ▢▢▢ Saudi Arabia.

4 🔊 4.6 Read and match. Then listen.

1 It is in the UK. It is not in Mexico. **b**

2 It is in the UAE. It is not in Greece. ☐

3 It is in Brazil. It is not in Saudi Arabia. ☐

5 Read and trace.

→ **1** I am   I **am** not   → **2** You are   You are not

→ **3** She is   She is not   → **4** He is   He is not

→ **5** It is   It is not   → **6** We are   We are not

→ **7** They are   They are not

6 Write.

> **NOTICE (!)**
> → It's = It is
> → It isn't = It is not = It's not
> → They're = They are
> → They aren't = They are not

1 It isn't in Turkey.

It _is_ _not_ in Turkey.

2 It's in the UK.

It _____ in the UK.

3 They're from Oman.

They _____ from Oman.

4 They aren't from Japan.

They _____ _____ from Japan.

7 4.7 Read and listen. Then write.

1 It _is_ _not_ in the UK.
It _____ in France.

2 It _____ _____ in Brazil.
It _____ in Mexico.

3 It _____ in Turkey.
It is not in Saudi Arabia.

8 Read and <u>underline</u> the countries. Then complete.

What is the country in the box? _____

Where in the world?

				F					
1	B	r		z		l			
2		m		n					
3	S		n	g		p		r	
4	G	r		c					
5	M		x		c				

Iguazu Falls

1 It is not in <u>Mexico</u>. It is in Brazil.

Bahla Fort

2 It is not in Saudi Arabia. It is in Oman.

Botanic Garden

3 It is not in Japan. It is in Singapore.

Santorini

4 It is not in France. It is in Greece.

Coba

5 It is not in Brazil. It is in Mexico.

9 Write **.** and the CAPITAL letters.

1 It is not in the UK. It is in Greece.

2 it is not in France it is in the UK

3 it is in Oman it is not in Saudi Arabia

4 it is in Japan it is not in Singapore

1 🔊 4.8 Listen and read. Trace. Then write.

1 → new
→ new

2 → old
→

3 → expensive
→

4 → cheap
→

5 → beautiful
→

6 → clean
→

2 🔊 4.9 Look at **1** and match. Then listen and say.

● | 1 | | | | ●●● ● | | ●●● ●

3 🔊 4.10 Read and circle. Then listen and check.

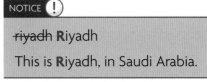

NOTICE ❗

~~riyadh~~ **R**iyadh
This is **R**iyadh, in Saudi Arabia.

1 This is Tokyo, in Japan. It is **cheap** / **expensive**.

2 This is Riyadh, in Saudi Arabia. It is **clean** / **old**.

3 This is Istanbul, in Turkey. It is **beautiful** / **new**.

4 Write the CAPITAL letters and ›.

T

1 This is ~~tokyo~~, in Japan. 2 This is doha in Qatar.

3 This is Istanbul, in turkey. 4 This is London in the uK.

5 4.11 Match and write. Then listen and check.

~~clean~~   beautiful   cheap   new   old   expensive

It is **c l e a n** and ▢▢▢▢▢▢▢▢▢ .

It is ▢▢▢ and ▢▢▢▢▢ .

It is ▢▢▢ and ▢▢▢▢▢▢▢▢ .

6 Writing Challenge Write about a city in your country.

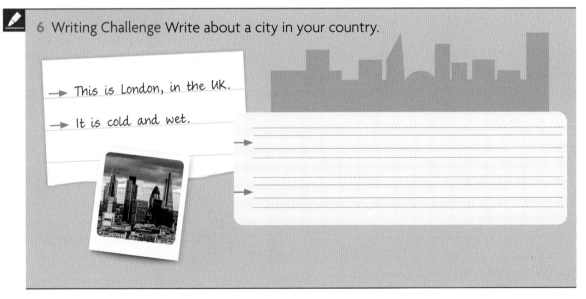

→ This is London, in the UK.

→ It is cold and wet.

SOUND AND SPELLING *e, ee, ea*

7 🔊 **4.12** Listen and read. Then trace.
Listen again and say.

→ He is in Greece. Greece

→ is cheap and clean.

8 🔊 **4.13** Listen and read. Then trace.
Listen again and say.

ea	**ee**	**e**
→ cheap	→ Greece	→ he
→ clean	→ three	→ she
→ easy	→	→
→	→	
→		

9 🔊 **4.14** Read. Then look at **8** and write. Listen and check.

bean   peel   seat   me   green

10 🔊 **4.15** Read and listen. Circle *e, ee, ea* words. Then say.

She is in Greece. Greece
is cheap and clean.

LANGUAGE FOCUS

1 🔊 **4.16** Read, listen and match.

→Who's this? ⟶ **2**
→His name is Saeed.

→What's this?
→It's a camel.

→Where's this?
→It's in Saudi Arabia.

2 Match. Then trace.

1   Where's this?

2   Who's this?

3   What's this?

Who is this?
What is this?
Where is this?

3 🔊 **4.17** Read and (circle). Then listen and check.

NOTICE ❗

Where's this? = Where is this?

1 **What / Where** is this? It is in the UAE.

2 **Who / What** is this? His name is Ahmed.

3 **What / Who** is this? It is a tent.

4 🔊 4.18 Read and match. Then listen and check.

desert

jeep

teacher

a

1

a	Where is this?	This is my teacher.
b	Who is this?	This is in the desert.
c	What is this?	This is his jeep.

sea

beach

family

b

2

a	Where is this?	This is my family.
b	Who is this?	This is the sea.
c	What is this?	This is on the beach.

5 Write the CAPITAL letters and ❓.

1 W̶here is this ?

2 who is this

3 what is this

SOUND AND SPELLING REVIEW

6 🔊 4.19 Listen and read. Then trace. Listen again and say.

1 → teacher   **2** → desert   **3** → jeep

4 → beach   **5** → family   **6** → sea

th **7** Spelling Challenge Cover **6** and write.

1 t e a cher   **2** d __ sert   **3** j __ __ p

4 b __ __ ch   **5** f __ mily   **6** s __ __

SOUND AND SPELLING *wh*

8 🔊 **4.20** Read and listen. Then trace.

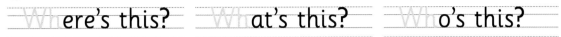

Where's this?   What's this?   Who's this?

9 🔊 **4.21** Look and listen. Then trace. Say.

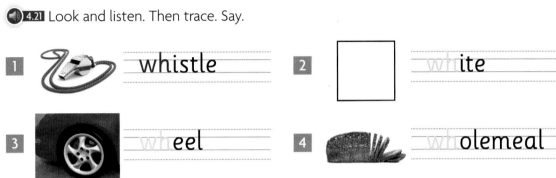

1 whistle   **2** white

3 wheel   **4** wholemeal

10 🔊 **4.22** Trace. Look at **9** and write. Then listen and check.

→ where   →   → who

→ what   →   →

→

11 🔊 **4.23** Listen and (circle). Then match. Listen again and check.

1 **What's / Where's** this?   It is in Japan.

2 **Who's / What's** this?   It is a whistle.

3 **Who's / Where's** this?   She is my teacher.

LISTENING FOCUS

1 🔊 **4.24** Look and (circle).
Then listen and check.

1	Where is the student?	in class / in the library
2	Where is the student from?	London / Jeddah

2 🔊 **4.25** Listen and read. Then match.

1	This is the desert.	*a*
2	This is the beach.	
3	This is the university.	

3 🔊 **4.26** Listen and match. Then listen and check.

1	This is the desert.	It's beautiful and clean.
2	This is the beach.	It's big and hot.
3	This is the university.	It's new. It's not old.

⊙ KEY WORDS FOR LITERACY

1 Read and circle.

1	**what** →	(what) →	when →	what →	at →	what
2	**who** →	how →	who →	when →	who →	now
3	**when** →	when →	hen →	were →	when →	when
4	**where** →	were →	here →	where →	were →	where

2 Cover and complete.

1	w h a t →	w h ▨ ▨ →	w ▨ ▨ ▨ →	▨ ▨ ▨ ▨
2	w h o →	w h ▨ →	w ▨ ▨ →	▨ ▨ ▨
3	w h e n →	w h ▨ ▨ →	w ▨ ▨ ▨ →	▨ ▨ ▨ ▨
4	w h e r e →	w h ▨ ▨ ▨ →	w ▨ ▨ ▨ ▨ →	▨ ▨ ▨ ▨ ▨

3 🔊 **4.27** Read and write. Then listen and check.

1 _____ is this?   It is in Japan.

fo mber

2 _____ is this?   It is a jeep.

	WEDNESDAY
MORNING	10:00

3 _____ is this?   It is on Wednesday morning.

4 _____ is this?   She is my teacher.

READING AND WRITING

1 Look and match.

1 car ☐   2 camera ☐   3 Tokyo ☐   4 Japan ☐

5 Asia ☐   6 students ☐

2 🔊 4.28 Read and ⟨circle⟩. Then read and listen.

cars   Asia   interesting   cameras   students
old   expensive   big   ~~Japan~~   beautiful

→ ⟨Japan⟩ is a country in Asia. Tokyo is a city in Japan. It is big and expensive.
→ It is not boring. It is interesting. Nissan cars are from Japan. Canon and Sony
→ cameras are from Japan. The Imperial Palace is in Tokyo. It is big and old.
→ Ueno Park is in Tokyo. It is clean and beautiful. Tokyo University is in Tokyo.
→ It is not new. It is old. Students study Japanese, Business and English.

3 🔊 4.29 Read and ⟨circle⟩. Listen and check. Then trace.

1 Japan is a   city / **country** .

2 Tokyo is a   city / country .

3 Tokyo is   boring / big .

4 Nissan   cameras / cars are from Japan.

5 Students study   Maths / Business .

4 Look and read. Write . and the CAPITAL letters.

→ 'London Eye – big, new'.

→ In my city:

→ London Eye

→ What is it like? big , new

→ the uk is a country it is cold and wet

→ london is a city in the uk it is interesting it is not boring

→ the London Eye is in london it is big and new

5 Look and write.

My country: _____ What is it like? _____
and _____ .
My city: _____ What is it like? It is _____ .
It is not _____ .
In my city: _____ What is it like? _____
and _____ .

6 Look at **4** and **5**. Write about a country, city and place.

→ _____ is a country. It is _____

→ and _____.

→ _____ is a city in _____.

→ It is _____ . It is not _____.

→ _____ is in _____.

→ It is _____ and _____.

UNIT 5 WORK

1 🔊 5.1 Listen and read. Then trace. Match.

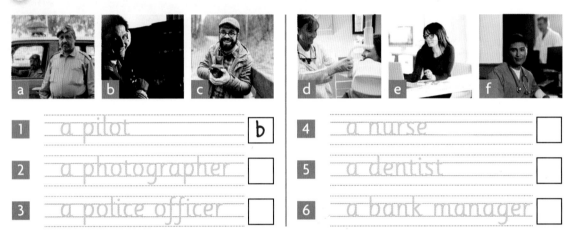

a	b	c
d	e	f

1	a pilot	b	4	a nurse	
2	a photographer		5	a dentist	
3	a police officer		6	a bank manager	

2 🔊 5.1 Look at 1. Match. Then listen again.

●   ●●   ●●●●   ●●●●   ●●●●●

☐   1 ☐   ☐   ☐   ☐

SOUND AND SPELLING f, ph, ff

3 🔊 5.2 Listen and read. Then trace. Listen again and say.

1	five	2	photographer
3	officer	4	family
5	phone	6	difficult

4 🔊 **5.3** Read and <u>underline</u>. Then listen and check.

Is he a photographer?

pilot

a →Yes, he is. / No, he isn't.

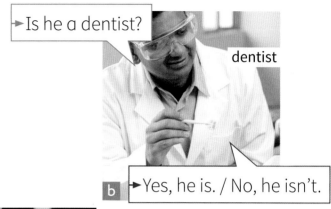

Is he a dentist?

dentist

b →Yes, he is. / No, he isn't.

Is she a police officer?

bank manager

c →Yes, she is. / No, she isn't.

5 Look at **4**. Read and match. Then trace.

1 **He is not a nurse. He is a dentist.**   b

2 **She is not a police officer. She is a bank manager.** ☐

3 **He is not a photographer. He is a pilot.** ☐

6 🔊 **5.4** Read and write *a*. Then listen and check.

1 She is ^*a* bank manager.

2 He is photographer.

3 She is not dentist.

4 He is not nurse.

> NOTICE ❗
> ⟶ a pilot = 1 pilot
> ⟶ He is a pilot.

7 🔊 **5.5** Find the words. Then listen and say.

1 He|is|a dentist.

2 Sheisnotanurse.

3 Sheisabankmanager.

4 Heisnotapoliceofficer.

8 🔊 **5.6** Listen. Then trace and write.

1. *police* o_____
2. d_____
3. b_____ m_____
4. p_____
5. p_____
6. n_____

9 Read and correct.

1. She is^*a* photographer.   *a*
2. He is police officer.
3. She a dentist.
4. He not a bank manager.
5. She is not nurse.

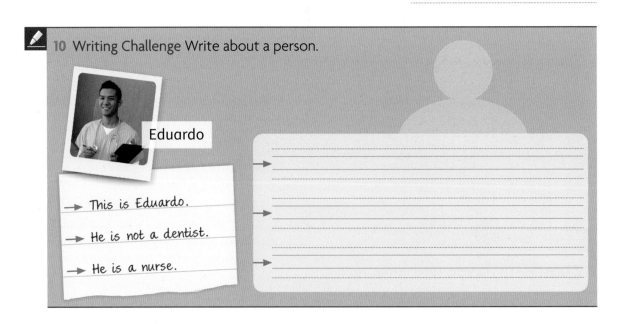

10 Writing Challenge Write about a person.

Eduardo

→ This is Eduardo.

→ He is not a dentist.

→ He is a nurse.

LISTENING AND READING 2

1 🔊 **5.7** Listen and read. Then trace. Match.

 a
 b
 c
 d
 e

1 → go to work [c]　2 → go to university [ ]

3 → go to the library [ ]　4 → go home [ ]

5 → meet friends [ ]

 f
 g
 h
 i

6 → start work [ ]　7 → start classes [ ]

8 → finish work [ ]　9 → finish classes [ ]

2 🔊 **5.8** Read and tick ✔. Then listen and check.

Sam
8:30	start work
5:30	finish work
6:00	meet friends

Ali
9:00	start classes
2:00	go to the library
5:00	go home

1 I study at university.　Sam [ ]　Ali [✔]

2 I work at a bank.　Sam [ ]　Ali [ ]

3 I start work at eight-thirty.　Sam [ ]　Ali [ ]

4 I start classes at nine o'clock.　Sam [ ]　Ali [ ]

5 I go home at five o'clock.　Sam [ ]　Ali [ ]

3 Read and match.

1 I finish classes   at university.

2 I go to the library   at a bank.

3 I study   at three o'clock.

4 I work   at one-thirty.

> NOTICE (!)
> → I study at university.
> → I work at a bank.
> → I go home at five o'clock.

4 Look at NOTICE. Read and (circle).

1 We (go) to the library.

2 They start work at nine o'clock.

3 I study at university.

4 They meet friends at five o'clock.

5 We work at a bank.

> NOTICE (!)
> → I <u>meet</u> friends.
> → We <u>work</u> at a bank.
> → They <u>go</u> home at two o'clock.

5 (◀) 5.9 Read and (circle). Then listen and read.

1 **nine**   We go to university at (nine) o'clock.

2 **go**   I go home at four o'clock.

3 **They**   They finish classes at three o'clock.

6 Cover and complete.

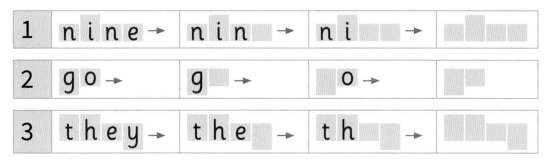

1	n i n e →	n i n →	n i →	
2	g o →	g →	o →	
3	t h e y →	t h e →	t h →	

7 Write the sentences.

1 start / work. / They / → _____They start work._____

2 go / We / home. → _____

3 I / at university. / study → _____

4 meet / They / friends. → _____

5 finish / We / work at six o'clock. → _____

8 Writing Challenge Complete the information.
Then write about your day.

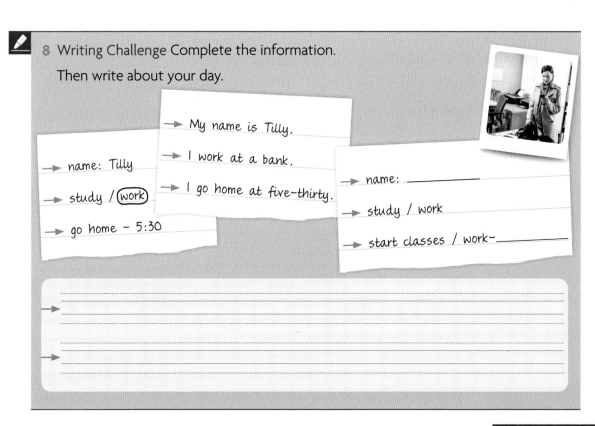

→ name: Tilly

→ study / (work)

→ go home – 5:30

→ My name is Tilly.

→ I work at a bank.

→ I go home at five-thirty.

→ name: _____

→ study / work

→ start classes / work– _____

1 🔊 **5.10** Look and match. Then listen.

 a
 b
 c
 d
 e
 f

1 meet people [e]   **2** take photographs [ ]

3 read emails [ ]   **4** travel to different countries [ ]

5 write emails [ ]   **6** help people [ ]

2 Read and complete.

1 t k photographs   **2** h l p people

3 w r t emails   **4** m t people in the city

5 r d emails   **6** t r v l to different countries

3 🔊 **5.11** Listen and match.

[5][ ]
 a

[ ][ ]
 b

[ ][ ]
 c

1 We help people.   **2** I meet people in the city.

3 They read emails.   **4** We travel to different countries.

5 I take photographs.   **6** They work in the city.

4 🔊 **5.12** Read and (circle). Then listen.

~~in the city~~   with people   on a computer

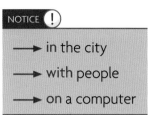

NOTICE ❗

→ in the city
→ with people
→ on a computer

→ Nancy is a bank manager. She works
→ (in the city). She works with people.
→ She works on a computer.

5 🔊 **5.13** Read and <u>underline</u>. Then listen and check. Trace.

→ Saeed works in the city. He works
→ on a computer. He writes emails.
→ He meets people.

1 → He ~~works / reads~~ **on a computer.**

2 → He ~~reads / writes~~ **emails.**

3 → He ~~meets / helps~~ **people.**

NOTICE ❗

→ He writes emails.
→ She meets people.

6 🔊 **5.14** Write **s**. Then listen and check.

1 He work**s** on a computer.

2 She travel to different countries.

3 He work with people.

4 She write emails.

5 She work in the city.

SOUND AND SPELLING adding s

7 🔊 **5.15** Read, listen and (circle).

| **1** **read** | She (reads) books. | **2** **write** | He writes emails. |

| **3** **finish** | She finishes at three-thirty. | **4** **study** | He studies English. |

| **5** **take** | He takes photographs. | **6** **help** | She helps people. |

8 🔊 **5.16** Look at **7** and write. Then listen and say.

+ s   + es   y + ies

→ _____reads_____   → _____   → _____

→ _____writes_____

→ _____

→ _____

9 🔊 **5.17** Listen and match. Write. Then listen again and say.

~~wash~~   finish   ~~washes~~   watch   finishes   watches

●   ●● | ●●   ●●●

→ _____wash_____   → _____washes_____ | → _____   → _____

→ _____   → _____

th **10** 🔊 **5.18** Spelling Challenge Complete. Listen and check. Then look at **8** and write.

ies

1 cry	He _____cries_____ .
2 wash	She _____ .
3 fly	It _____ .
4 watch	He _____ .

LANGUAGE FOCUS

1 🔊 **5.19** Listen and read. Then trace. Listen again and say.

→ January	→ February	→ March	→ April
→ May	→ June	→ July	→ August
→ September	→ October	→ November	→ December

2 🔊 **5.20** Listen and write. Then say.

●	●●	●●●
→ M**arch**	→ A_____	→ S_____
→ J_____	→ A_____	→ O_____
→ M_____	●●●●	→ N_____
●●	→ J_____	→ D_____
→ J_____	→ F_____	

3 Look and match.

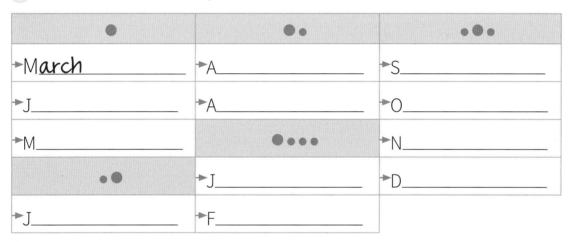

NOTICE ❗
→ July   ~~july~~
→ August   ~~august~~

1 first day of January	b	**2** Maths exam	☐
3 summer holiday	☐	**4** winter holiday	☐

4 Read and circle.

UNIVERSITY

→ August	first day
→ March	Business exam
→ May	IT exam
→ June	summer holiday

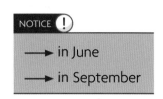

NOTICE ❗

→ in June

→ in September

1 When is the first day of university? in April / (in August) / in September

2 When is the Business exam? in March / in May / in June

3 When is the IT exam? in February / in March / in May

4 When is the summer holiday? in January / in June / in July

5 Write the CAPITAL letters.

1 ~~t~~(T)he summer holiday is in ~~a~~(A)ugust.

2 the first day of university is in october.

3 the English exam is in may.

4 the History exam is in april.

6 🔊 **5.21** Read and complete. Then listen and check.

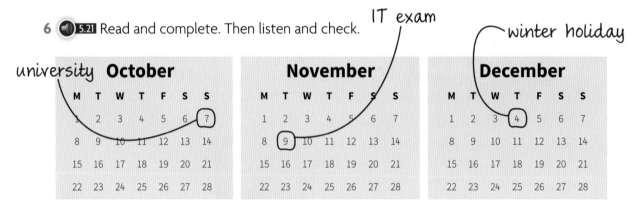

IT exam

winter holiday

university **October**

M	T	W	T	F	S	S
1	2	3	4	5	6	(7)
8	9	10	11	12	13	14
15	16	17	18	19	20	21
22	23	24	25	26	27	28

November

M	T	W	T	F	S	S
1	2	3	4	5	6	7
8	(9)	10	11	12	13	14
15	16	17	18	19	20	21
22	23	24	25	26	27	28

December

M	T	W	T	F	S	S
1	2	3	(4)	5	6	7
8	9	10	11	12	13	14
15	16	17	18	19	20	21
22	23	24	25	26	27	28

1 The first day of university is __in October__ .

2 The IT exam is _____ .

3 The winter holiday is _____ .

SOUND AND SPELLING *ou*

7 🔊 **5.22** Listen and read. Then trace. Listen again and say.

You teach four classes in our country.

8 🔊 **5.23** Listen. Then match. Listen again and say.

group   cloud   young   four

1 our ———————————— group
2 course   cloud
3 you   young
4 country   four

9 🔊 **5.24** Listen. Then write. Listen again and say.

    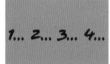

house   your   mouth   double   count

fourteen   pound   youth   shout

our   course   you   country
  house   _____   _____   _____

_____   _____

_____

_____

_____

LISTENING FOCUS

1 Look and match.

a   b   c

| **1** | work at night | b | | **2** | teachers | ☐ | | **3** | businesswoman | ☐ |

2 🔊 **5.25** Listen and (circle) Yes or No.

1	Asma travels to different countries.	(Yes)	No
2	She starts work at nine o'clock.	Yes	No
3	Peter is from Turkey.	Yes	No
4	He is a police officer.	Yes	No
5	Metin and Ahmet are from the UK.	Yes	No
6	They meet interesting people.	Yes	No

3 Write **.** and the CAPITAL letters.

1 ~~a~~ A smaller is from the ~~uae~~ UAE. S she is a businesswoman **.**

2 peter works at night he helps people

3 they are teachers they finish classes at two-thirty

⊙ KEY WORDS FOR LITERACY

1 🔊 **5.26** Read and ⟨circle⟩. Then listen.

1	**with**	He works with students.
2	**we**	We take photographs.
3	**work**	He works at night.
4	**write**	They write emails.

2 Read and ⟨circle⟩.

1 **with**	→ ⟨with⟩	→ when	→ with	→ what	→ with
2 **we**	→ we	→ when	→ be	→ he	→ we
3 **work**	→ wore	→ word	→ work	→ work	→ word
4 **write**	→ wrote	→ write	→ wright	→ write	→ wrote

3 Cover and complete.

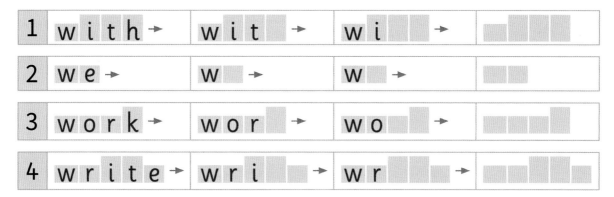

1 w i t h → w i t □ → w i □ □ → □□□□

2 w e → w □ → w □ → □□

3 w o r k → w o r □ → w o □ □ → □□□□

4 w r i t e → w r i □ □ → w r □ □ □ → □□□□□

4 🔊 **5.27** Read and write. Then listen and check.

1 They _ _ _ _ _ emails.

2 She works _ _ _ _ nurses.

3 I _ _ _ _ with pilots.

4 _ _ finish work at five o'clock.

1 🔊 **5.28** Look and match. Then read and (circle). Listen and read.

a   b   c

1 choose a job **b**   **2** write work emails ☐

3 speak in a meeting ☐

WHAT DO YOU WANT TO BE?

a pilot · a dentist · a photographer · a nurse · a business person
a police officer · a teacher

'ENGLISH FOR WORK' CLASSES

→ **When?** Mondays and Wednesdays   → In this class, we study:

→ **What time?** 3:30–5:00   → • how to (choose a job)

→ **Where?** Room 11   → • how to write work emails

        → • how to speak in a meeting

→ The classes are with Mrs Hassan. They start in September. The exam is in December.

→ Email address: jobclasses@uni.ac

2 Look at **1**. Read again and match.

1	The classes are on	three-thirty.
2	The classes start at	five o'clock.
3	The classes finish at	room 11.
4	The classes are in	December.
5	The teacher is	Mondays and Wednesdays.
6	The exam is in	Mrs Hassan.

3 🔊 **5.29** Read and correct. Write. Then listen and check.

at   in   a   at   on   with

at
1 The classes start^ten-thirty.   ___*at*___

2 He wants to be police officer.   _____

3 The English exam is March.   _____

4 She works a bank.   _____

5 He works people.   _____

6 He works a computer.   _____

4 Write about your friend.

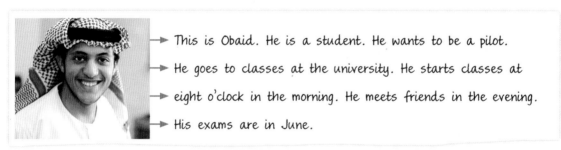

→ This is Obaid. He is a student. He wants to be a pilot.
→ He goes to classes at the university. He starts classes at
→ eight o'clock in the morning. He meets friends in the evening.
→ His exams are in June.

→ This is _____. _____ is a student.

→ _____ wants to be _____.

→ _____ goes to classes at _____.

→ _____ starts classes at _____ _____ in

→ the morning. _____ _____ _____ in the

→ evening. The exams are _____

→ _____.

UNIT 6 · FOOD AND HEALTH

LISTENING AND READING 1

1 🔊 **6.1** Listen and read. Then trace and write. Listen again and say.

1
drink

drink   drink

2
juice

juice

3
coffee

coffee

4
water

water

5
tea

tea

6
eat

eat

7
bread

bread

8
rice

rice

9
cheese

cheese

10
salad

salad

11
fish

fish

12
meat

meat

13
fruit

fruit

14
vegetables

vegetables

UNLOCK **BASIC** LITERACY

2 🔊 **6.2** Listen. Look at **1** and write.

●		●●	●●●
drink e _ _ m_ _ _ _		coffee	
f_ _ _ j_ _ _ _		s_ _ _ _	v _ _ _ _ _ _ _ _ _ _ s
r_ _ _ f_ _ _ _		w_ _ _ _	
ch _ _ _ _ t_ _			
br _ _ _			

SOUND AND SPELLING REVIEW

3 🔊 **6.3** <u>Underline</u> and (circle). Then listen and say.

1 big   rice / (fish)

2 hot   coffee / bread

3 five   rice / fruit

4 brother   drink / bread

5 friend   fruit / fish

4 🔊 **6.4** Listen and read. Then say.

1

I eat vegetables.

2

I do not eat salad.

3

I drink water.

4

I do not drink juice.

5 🔊 **6.5** Listen and match.

Huda   Tariq   Natasha

6 Read and write.

NOTICE ❗

🔊 I don't eat rice.   ✏️ I do not eat rice.

1 → I **don't** eat bread.   I ____do____ ____not____ eat bread.

2 → I **don't** drink water.   I _____ _____ drink water.

3 → I **don't** eat cheese.   I _____ _____ eat cheese.

4 → I **don't** drink tea.   I _____ _____ drink tea.

7 🔊 **6.6** Write the sentences. Then listen and check.

1 eat / rice. / I   I eat rice. _____

2 fish. / I / eat   _____

3 I / tea. / drink   _____

4 do not / I / bread. / eat   _____

5 drink / juice. / do not / I   _____

LISTENING AND READING 2

1 🔊 **6.7** Read and complete. Then listen and say.

> lunch   ~~to bed~~   up   to work   breakfast   dinner   to university

 go **to bed**

 have ▢▢▢▢▢▢

 have ▢▢▢▢▢

 walk ▢▢ ▢▢▢▢▢▢▢ ▢

 have ▢▢▢▢▢ ▢▢▢▢

 get ▢▢

 drive ▢▢ ▢▢▢▢▢

2 🔊 **6.8** Listen and read. Then trace. Listen again and say.

→ This is Eissa. He *gets up* at seven-thirty.

→ He *doesn't walk* to university. He drives to

→ university. He *has* lunch with friends at twelve

→ o'clock. He *doesn't have* dinner with his friends.

→ He *has* dinner with his family at eight o'clock.

→ He *goes* to bed at ten-thirty.

3 Look at NOTICE. Read and write.

1 | He **doesn't** get up at six o'clock.

He ___does___ ___not___ get up at six o'clock.

2 | They **don't** walk to university.

They _____ _____ walk to university.

3 | She **doesn't** drive to work.

She _____ _____ drive to work.

4 | He **doesn't** have dinner at six-thirty.

He _____ _____ have dinner at six-thirty.

4 🔊 **6.9** Read and write. Then listen and check.

My day by Eissa Ahmad

7:30	get up
8:00	have breakfast
9:30	go to university
12:00	have lunch
3:30	finish classes
11:00	go to bed

NOTICE ❗

I walk to university. 🚶✓
🔊 I don't walk to university. 🚶✗
✏️ I do not walk to university.
He walks to university. 🚶✓
🔊 He doesn't walk to university. 🚶✗
✏️ He does not walk to university.

1 Eissa ___gets up___ at seven-thirty.

2 He ___does not have___ breakfast at nine o'clock.

3 He _____ to university at ten-thirty.

4 He _____ lunch at twelve o'clock.

5 He _____ classes at two-thirty.

6 He _____ to bed at eleven o'clock.

5 🔊 6.10 Read and (circle). Then listen and check.

1 **do**   I (do) not eat fish.

2 **goes** He goes to bed at ten o'clock.

3 **has**   She has lunch at one-thirty.

4 **up**   I get up at six-thirty.

5 **does** He does not eat meat.

6 Look. Then cover and complete.

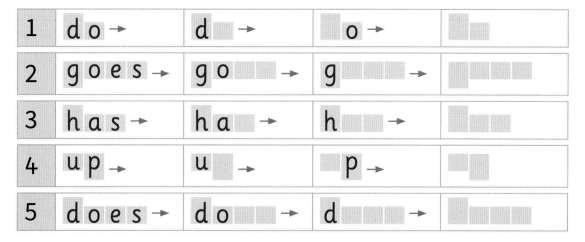

7 Writing Challenge Write about your friend.

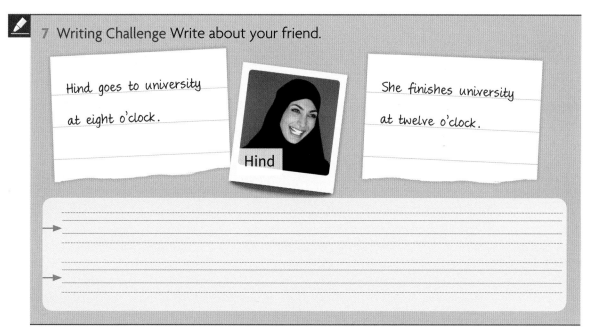

Hind goes to university at eight o'clock.

Hind

She finishes university at twelve o'clock.

1. **6.11** Listen and read. Then say.

 1 green tea

 2 go to bed late

 3 red meat

 4 fruit and vegetables

 5 get up early

 6 milk and sugar

2. **6.12** Read and complete. Then listen and check.

> green tea   fruit and vegetables   ~~red meat~~
> to bed late   get up early   milk and sugar

The UK

78% A lot of people eat **r e d   m e a t**.

41% Some people go ▢▢ ▢▢▢▢ ▢▢▢▢.

12% Not a lot of people drink ▢▢▢▢▢ ▢▢▢▢.

Japan

9% Not a lot of people drink coffee with

▢▢▢▢ ▢▢▢ ▢▢▢▢▢.

38% Some people ▢▢▢ ▢▢ ▢▢▢▢.

81% A lot of people eat

▢▢▢▢▢ ▢▢▢ ▢▢▢▢▢▢▢▢▢.

> **NOTICE !**
>
> A lot of
> = ●●●●●●●●●○
>
> Some
> = ●●●●●○○○○○
>
> Not a lot of
> = ●●○○○○○○○○

3 🔊 6.13 Read and circle. Listen and check. Then write.

1 99% _____**A lot of**_____ people eat red meat.
(A lot of / Some / Not a lot of)

2 3% _____ people drink coffee
(A lot of / Some / Not a lot of)

with milk and sugar.

3 92% _____ people eat
(A lot of / Some / Not a lot of)

fruit and vegetables.

4 47% _____ people go to bed late.
(A lot of / Some / Not a lot of)

4 🔊 6.14 Find the words. Then listen and check.

1 Not|a|lotofpeopleeatredmeat.

2 Somepeopledrinkcoffeewithmilk.

3 Somepeopledrinkgreentea.

4 AlotofpeopleinSpaineatfruit.

✏️ **5** Writing Challenge Write about your country.

A lot of people drink juice.

The UK

Not a lot of people drink green tea.

6 🔊 **6.15** Listen and read. Then trace. Listen again and say.

1 We eat meat for dinner.

2 He drinks green tea and coffee.

3 She eats cheese and fish.

7 🔊 **6.16** Match and write. Listen and check. Then say.

~~meat~~   fish   tea   me   coffee   he   green   dinner

1 **ea**t   ch**ee**se   w**e**   _m e a t_ ___ __

___ ___ __ _____

2 dr**i**nk ____ _____

th **8** 🔊 **6.17** Spelling Challenge Listen and write *ee*, *ea* or *i*.

D _i_ nner menu

f __ sh and ch __ ps

ch __ __ se

gr __ __ n t __ __

MENU

LANGUAGE FOCUS

1 🔊 **6.18** Listen and read. Then trace. Listen again and say.

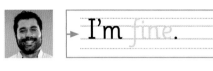 I'm fine.    I'm busy.

 I'm tired.    I'm great.

 I'm not well.    I'm hungry.

2 🔊 **6.19** Match and write. Listen and check. Then say.

| not | fine | hungry | well | ~~bad~~ | tired |

1 b**a**g ___*bad*___   **2** h**o**t _____

3 w**e**t _____   **4** b**u**s _____

5 n**i**n**e** _____ _____

3 🔊 **6.20** Listen. Then write. Listen again and check.

| well | fine | hungry | not bad | busy | tired |

1 **A:** Hello, Mr Martin. How are you?

   B: I'm ___ ___ ___ ___. How are you?

   A: I'm not ___ ___ ___.

   B: I'm sorry.

   > NOTICE ❗
   >
   > not bad 😃 = well
   >
   > I'm not bad. = I'm well.

2 **A:** Hi, Amna. How are you?

   B: I'm ___ ___ ___ ___ ___! How are you?

   A: I'm ___ ___ ___.

4 🔊 6.21 Read and match. Then listen and check.

1 Muna is busy. **2** Megan and Jess are tired. **3** Yousif is hungry. **4** I am great.

a ☐ They walk to university. **b** ☐ He needs his lunch.

c ☐ I have interesting classes. **d** ☐ She has a lot of classes.

5 Read and (circle). Draw →.

1 (Jack) is tired. (He) walks to work.

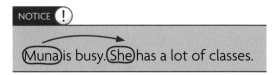

NOTICE ❗

(Muna) is busy. (She) has a lot of classes.

2 Julie and Shamsa are fine. They finish classes at one-thirty.

3 Lidia is busy. She has a lot of classes.

4 Hussain is not hungry. He is not well.

6 Read and write.

    I   They   She   you

●●●

From: eman@college.ac.ae   Reply   Forward

Date: 17 June

Hi Dalia,

How are _____ ?

I am not bad. _____ finish classes at three o'clock.
Some students are busy. _____ have a lot of classes.
Our teacher is Mrs Locke. _____ is great!

Best wishes,

Eman

SOUND AND SPELLING -nk, -st, -nch

7 🔊 **6.22** Listen and read. Then trace. Listen again and say.

I dri nk coffee at breakfa st and I dri nk tea at lu nch .

8 🔊 **6.23** Listen and read. Then trace. Listen again and say.

1	ba nk	i nk	pla nk
2	fa st	ve st	fir st
3	Fre nch	bra nch	be nch

9 🔊 **6.24** Listen and write.

		nk	st/nch	
1		li _ _	li _ _	
2		mi _ _	mi _ _	
3		pi _ _	pi _ _ _	

10 🔊 **6.25** Look at **9**. Listen and circle.

1 🔊 6.26 Listen. Then write.

Student survey – healthy eating
1   e a t fruit and vegetables
2   eat red m _ _ _ t
3   d r _ _ n k coffee
4   g _ _ t up early
5   walk to _ _ n _ v _ rs _ ty
6   go to bed l _ _ t _

2 🔊 6.27 Listen and match. Then listen and check.

A lot of students	Some students	Not a lot of students
2 ☐	☐ ☐	☐ ☐

1 eat red meat
2 drink coffee with milk
3 get up early
4 eat fruit and vegetables
5 walk to university
6 go to bed late

3 🔊 6.28 Listen and ⟨circle⟩. Then listen and check.

1 **(Not a lot of)** / **A lot of** students drink green tea.

2 **Some** / **Not a lot of** students eat bread and rice.

3 **A lot of** / **Some** students drink juice.

4 **Some** / **A lot of** students work in the library.

5 **A lot of** / **Not a lot of** students have dinner at university.

6 **Not a lot of** / **Some** students go to bed early.

⊙ KEY WORDS FOR LITERACY

1 🔊 **6.29** Read and ⟨circle⟩. Then listen and check.

1	**of**	A lot of students drink green tea.
2	**some**	Some students eat bread and rice.
3	**lot**	A lot of students work in the library.
4	**not**	Not a lot of students go to bed late.

2 Look and ⟨circle⟩.

1	**of**	→	at	→	⟨of⟩	→	of	→	if	→	on
2	**some**	→	same	→	some	→	soon	→	some	→	seem
3	**lot**	→	lot	→	tot	→	top	→	lot	→	lot
4	**not**	→	not	→	lot	→	now	→	note	→	not

3 Look. Then cover and complete.

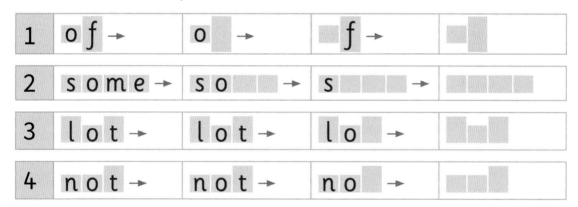

4 🔊 **6.30** Read and write. Then listen and check.

1 Not a _____ of people go to bed late.

2 _____ people have dinner at two o'clock.

3 A lot _____ people walk to work.

4 _____ a lot of people in Japan eat red meat.

1 🔊 6.31 Look and match. Then listen, read and check.

1 fruit and vegetables **2** sugar **3** cheese

FOOD AND HEALTH
HEALTHY EATING

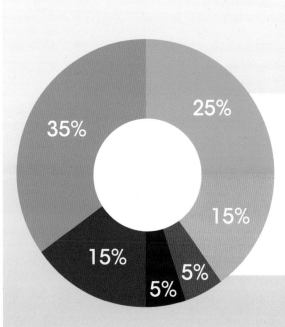

Bread and rice ☐

☐

Red meat

☐

Fish

☐

Healthy people eat a lot of fruit and vegetables. They eat a lot of bread and rice. They do not eat a lot of red meat. They do not eat a lot of sugar. They eat some cheese. They eat some fish.

2 Look at **1**. Read and write.

Healthy people:
- eat _____ fruit and vegetables.
- eat a lot of _____ .
- do not eat _____ red meat.
- do not eat a lot of _____ .
- eat _____ cheese.
- eat some _____ .

3 🔊 **6.32** Look. Then read and complete. Listen and check.

Unhealthy eating: an example

Some people are not healthy.

Rashid is a student in the USA. He **e a t s a l o t o f** red meat.

He ▨▨▨▨ ▨▨▨ ▨▨▨ ▨ ▨▨▨ ▨▨ fruit and

vegetables. He ▨▨▨▨▨ ▨ ▨▨▨ ▨▨ juice with sugar.

He ▨▨▨▨ not ▨▨▨▨▨ ▨ ▨▨▨ ▨▨ green

tea. He ▨▨▨▨ ▨▨▨▨▨ cheese.

4 🔊 **6.33** Read and circle. Correct. Then listen and check.

1 She eat a lot of bread. _____ *eats* _____

2 He do not eat cheese. _____

3 She does not drinks milk. _____

5 Write about your friend.

eat	drink
a lot of _____	a lot of _____
some _____	some _____
✗ _____	✗ _____

My friend eats a lot of _____ . _____

_____ some _____ . _____ does

not _____ _____ .

_____ drinks a lot of _____ .

_____ drinks _____ _____ .

_____ _____ _____ drink

_____ .

LISTENING AND READING 1

1 🔊 **7.1** Listen and read. Then trace. Listen again and say.

1   a park

2   a hospital

3   a train station

4   a beach

5   a shopping centre

6   an office building

7   an airport

2 🔊 **7.2** Listen, read and match.

☐1 shopping   ☐ airport   ☐ hospital   ☐ building

1 ●●   2 ●●●

3 Read and complete.

office building   train station   hospital
airport   shopping centre   park

Nadia, Dubai

Nadia: I live in Dubai. I live near an **o f f i c e b u i l d i n g**

and a ▢▢▢▢▢ ▢▢▢▢▢ .

I do not live near a ▢▢▢▢▢▢ .

Andy, London

Andy: I live in London. I live near a **p a r k** and a ▢▢▢▢

▢▢▢▢▢▢ . I do not live near an ▢▢▢▢▢▢ .

4 🔊 **7.3** Read **3** again. Circle *a* and *an*. Then listen.

5 🔊 **7.4** Write the sentences. Then listen and check.

NOTICE ❗

a park	a beach
an airport	an office building

1 a beach / near / I live / and a park.
   I live near a beach and a park.

2 I live / a hospital / near / and an airport.
   _____

3 I / live / do not / near / a shopping centre.
   _____

4 I / near / live / do not / an office building.
   _____

SOUND AND SPELLING *-rt, -rk*

6 🔊 **7.5** Listen and read. Then trace. Listen again.

The park is near the airport.

7 🔊 **7.6** Listen and read. Then trace. Listen again and say.

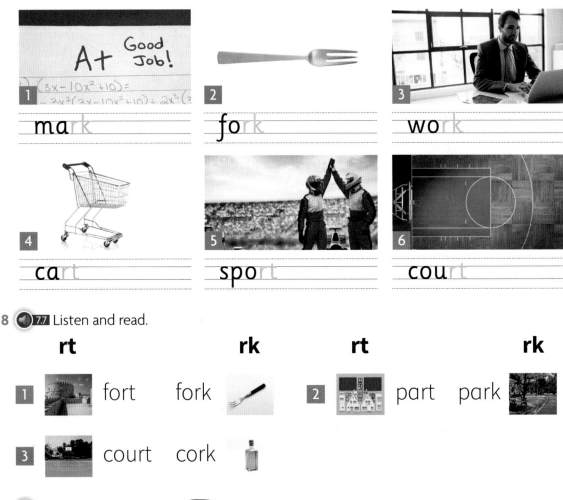

1 mark

2 fork

3 work

4 cart

5 sport

6 court

8 🔊 **7.7** Listen and read.

rt	**rk**		**rt**	**rk**

1   fort   fork

2   part   park

3   court   cork

9 🔊 **7.8** Look at **8**. Listen and (circle).

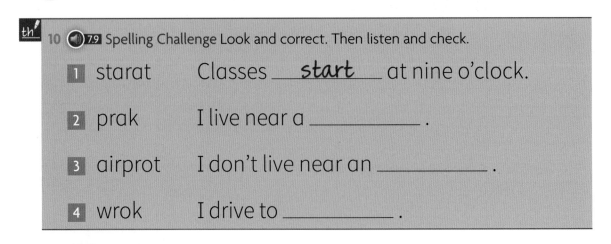

th'   **10** 🔊 **7.9** Spelling Challenge Look and correct. Then listen and check.

1   starat   Classes ___**start**___ at nine o'clock.

2   prak   I live near a _____.

3   airprot   I don't live near an _____.

4   wrok   I drive to _____.

LISTENING AND READING 2

1 🔊 **7.10** Look and complete. Then listen and check.

| a house   a factory   a hotel   ~~a restaurant~~   a shop |

a r e s t a u r a n t

SOUND AND SPELLING REVIEW

2 🔊 **7.11** Match and write. Then listen and check.

a restaurant **b** ~~factory~~ **c** hotel **d** shop
e house **f** hospital **g** beach **h** shopping
i centre **j** office

1 b**a**g | b | _factory_

2 r**e**d | | _____ | | _____

3 h**o**t | | _____ | | _____

| | _____ | | _____

4 m**ea**t | | _____

5 ph**o**n**e** | | _____

6 **ou**r | | _____

3 🔊 **7.12** Read and listen. Listen and (circle). Trace.

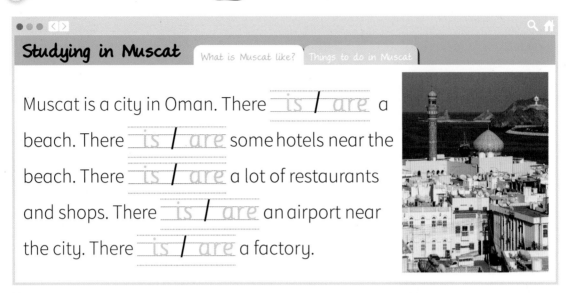

Studying in Muscat   What is Muscat like?   Things to do in Muscat

Muscat is a city in Oman. There ~~is / are~~ a beach. There ~~is / are~~ some hotels near the beach. There ~~is / are~~ a lot of restaurants and shops. There ~~is / are~~ an airport near the city. There ~~is / are~~ a factory.

4 🔊 **7.13** Find the words. Then listen and check.

1 | Therearealotofhotels.
2 | Thereisafactoryandanairport.
3 | Therearesomefactoriesandshops.
4 | Thereisanairportnearthecity.
5 | Therearealotofbeachesandtwouniversities.

> NOTICE ❗
> There is a train station.
> There are some hotels.

5 🔊 **7.14** Trace. Then listen and say.

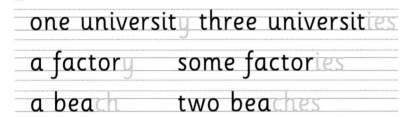

one university   three universities
a factory   some factories
a beach   two beaches

> NOTICE ❗
> one beach –
> three beaches
> a university –
> some universities

6 Look and (circle).

1 **live**	(live)	life	live	five	live
2 **a**	an	a	a	an	a
3 **an**	and	a	an	an	a
4 **there**	there	the	here	there	then

7 Look. Then cover and complete.

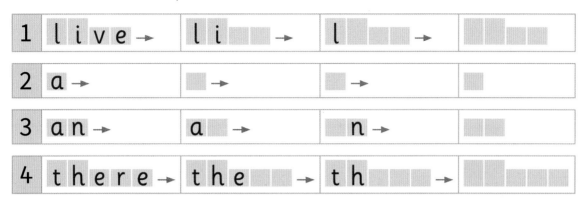

1	l i v e →	l i ▭ ▭ →	l ▭ ▭ ▭ →	▭ ▭ ▭ ▭
2	a →	▭ →	▭ →	▭
3	a n →	a ▭ →	▭ n →	▭ ▭
4	t h e r e →	t h e ▭ ▭ →	t h ▭ ▭ ▭ →	▭ ▭ ▭ ▭ ▭

8 🔊 7.15 Read and write. Then listen and check.

live   a   an   There

1 I don't _____ near a shop.

2 There is _____ airport.

3 _____ are some houses.

4 I live near _____ beach.

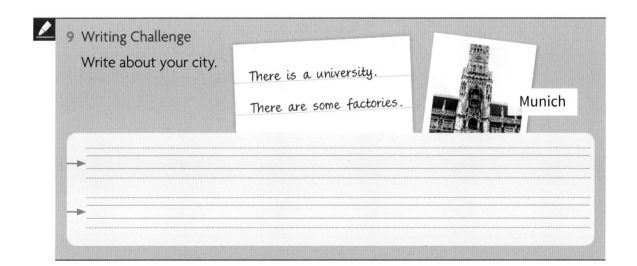

9 Writing Challenge

Write about your city.

There is a university.

There are some factories.

Munich

1 🔊 **7.16** Read and match. Listen and check. Trace.

a b c (1)

d e f

1	**tall buildings**	2	old streets
3	beautiful beaches	4	a famous stadium
5	an interesting market	6	a busy square

2 🔊 **7.17** Listen and look. Copy.

	tall	old
●	*t a l l*	_ _ _
	streets _ _ _ _ _ _ _	square _ _ _ _ _ _
●●	buildings _ _ _ _ _ _ _ _ _	beaches _ _ _ _ _ _ _
	busy _ _ _ _ _	market _ _ _ _ _ _ _
	famous _ _ _ _ _ _	
●●●	beautiful _ _ _ _ _ _ _ _ _	stadium _ _ _ _ _ _ _
	interesting _ _ _ _ _ _ _ _ _ _ _	

3 🔊 7.18 Read and match. Then listen and check.

| | | | a | | |

►I live in Dublin. It is an old city. There is a famous university. There are a lot of interesting streets.

►I live in Singapore. It is a new city. There are a lot of tall buildings. There is a famous park.

4 🔊 7.19 Read and complete. Then listen and check.

> new buildings   old library   interesting city   famous stadiums

I live in Manchester. It is an ▇▇▇▇▇▇ ▇▇▇▇ .

There are a lot of ▇▇▇ ▇▇▇▇▇▇ . There are two

▇▇▇▇▇▇ ▇▇▇▇▇▇ .

There is an ▇▇▇ ▇▇▇▇▇ .

library

5 🔊 7.20 Read and add the words. Then listen and check.

1	new	It is a ^new^ city.
2	busy	There is a square.
3	tall	There are some buildings.
4	old	There are a lot of houses.
5	famous	There is a stadium.

6 Writing Challenge Write about a city in your country.

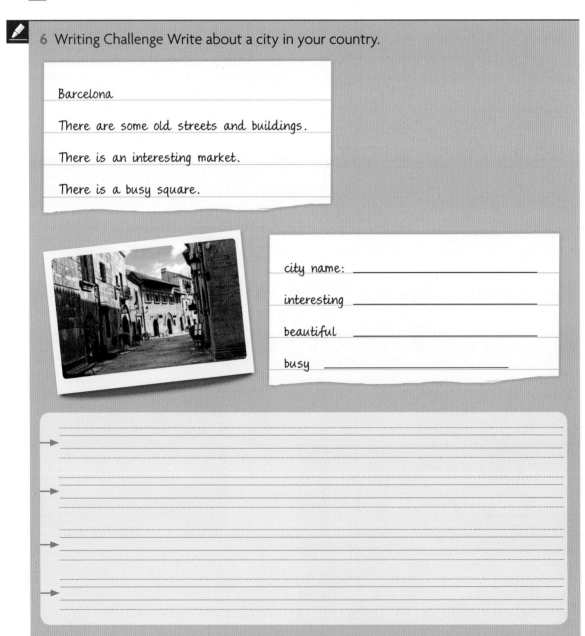

Barcelona

There are some old streets and buildings.

There is an interesting market.

There is a busy square.

city name: _____

interesting _____

beautiful _____

busy _____

LANGUAGE FOCUS

1 🔊 7.21 Listen and read. Then trace. Listen again.

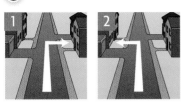

1 on the right

2 on the left

3 on Heaton Street

4 next to the office building

5 between the stadium and the park

6 near the shopping centre

2 🔊 7.22 Find the words. Listen and check. Look and match.

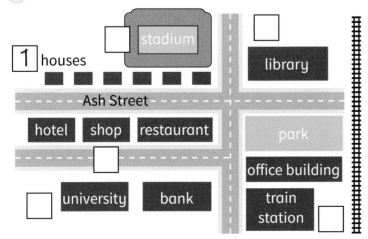

1 Thehousesareon AshStreet.

2 Thetrainstationisnearthepark.

3 Thelibraryisontheright.

4 Thestadiumisontheleft.

5 Theuniversityisnexttothebank.

6 Theshopisbetweenthehotel andtherestaurant.

3 🔊 **7.23** Read and add the words. Then listen and check.

1. on   My house is ^on Main Street.

2. between   The hotel is the restaurant and the shops.

3. next to   The park is the university.

4. near   The airport is the stadium.

5. on   The shops are the right.

4 🔊 **7.24** Write the sentences. Then listen and check.

1. the houses. / The stadium / next to / is

   The stadium is next to the houses.

2. is / the shops. / The market / near

   _____

3. The office buildings / the left. / on / are

   _____

4. between / the bank / The university / and the park. / is

   _____

5. Renton Street. / on / is / The shopping centre

   _____

SOUND AND SPELLING *st, tr, str*

5 🔊 **7.25** Listen and read. Then trace. Listen again and say.

st ation   tr ain   str eet

6 🔊 **7.26** Listen and read. Then trace. Listen again and say.

The tr ain st ation is on this str eet.

7 🔊 **7.27** Listen and read. Then trace. Listen again and say.

1

st udent

st airs

st ar

2

tr ee

tr affic

tr olley

3

str ong

str ing

str aight

8 🔊 **7.28** Spelling Challenge Look and correct. Then listen and check.

1 tirain _____ *train* _____   **2** satation _____

3 setreet _____   **4** sutednt _____

LISTENING FOCUS

1 ◉ 7.29 Listen and number, *1* and *2*.

Tsukiji fish market ☐   Dubai Mall ☐

2 ◉ 7.30 Look and match. Then listen and check.

market   shopping centre   busy   big   new   famous

_____   _____

_____   _____

_____   _____

3 ◉ 7.29 Look, listen again and (circle).

DUBAI MALL
- big and new
- a lot of shops with cameras, computers (bags)/ **books** and mobile phones
- restaurants from different **cities** / **countries**, some cheap
- tall **building** / **bank**

TSUJIKI FISH MARKET
- in Tokyo
- starts at **4:00** / **5:00** o'clock
- a lot of **big** / **small** shops
- some restaurants
- eat fish
- drink **coffee** / **green tea**

SOUND AND SPELLING REVIEW

4 ◉ 7.31 Match and write. Then listen and say.

~~shop~~   green   drink   cheap   there
great   with   phone   fish

1 sh ___shop___ _____   **2** ch _____

3 ph _____   **4** th _____ _____

5 gr _____   **6** dr _____

⊙ KEY WORDS FOR LITERACY

1 🔊 **7.32** Read and (circle). Then listen and check.

   1 **new**   There are a lot of (new) buildings.

   2 **old**   There is an old factory.

   3 **between**   The shops are between the restaurant and the bank.

   4 **to**   He drives to work.

2 Look and (circle).

1 **new**	→ (new)	→ now	→ new	→ none	→ new
2 **old**	→ cold	→ old	→ oil	→ old	→ old
3 **between**	→ behave	→ be two	→ between	→ be clean	→ between
4 **to**	→ two	→ two	→ too	→ to	→ to

3 Look. Then cover and complete.

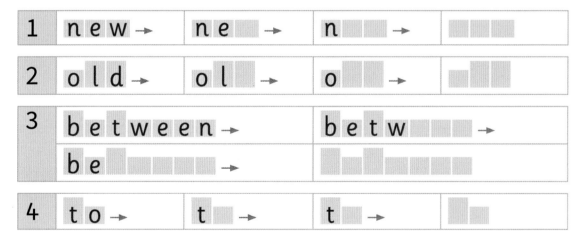

| 1 | n e w → | n e ▯ → | n ▯▯ → | ▯▯▯▯ |
| 2 | o l d → | o l ▯ → | o ▯▯ → | ▯▯▯ |

3 b e t w e e n →   b e t w ▯▯▯ →
    b e ▯▯▯▯▯▯ →

| 4 | t o → | t ▯ → | t ▯ → | ▯▯ |

4 🔊 **7.33** Listen and write. Then listen and check.

  1 The university is next _____ the stadium.

  2 There is a _____ shopping centre.

  3 The hospital is _____ the park and the train station.

  4 There is an _____ train station.

READING AND WRITING

1 🔊 **7.34** Read and write. Then read, listen and check.

> students   university   teachers

● ● ● ⟨ ⟩   🔍 🏠

HOME | COURSES | TIMETABLE   🔍 Search

1 The _____

The university is new and famous. It is near the desert. There is a beautiful park next to the university. There are big buildings and new classrooms. There is a great library. It has a lot of books and computers.

2 The _____

There are 2,500 students. They study IT, Business, Maths and English. The students are from different cities. There are cheap shops and restaurants for the students.

3 The _____

There are 150 teachers. A lot of teachers are from different countries. They live in houses at the university. The houses are near the classrooms.

2 Read. Write ✔ or ✘.

1 The university is old.   ✘

2 The university is next to a park.   ☐

3 There are small buildings.   ☐

4 The library has a lot of computers.   ☐

5 There are 2,500 students.   ☐

6 The students study History.   ☐

7 There are expensive shops.   ☐

8 There are 100 teachers.   ☐

9 The teachers live in houses at the university.   ☐

10 The houses are next to the classrooms.   ☐

3 🔊 7.35 Read and (circle). Correct. Then listen and check.

1 The university is (the park next to). __next to the park__

2 There is some good restaurants. _____

3 There are a lot of beautiful beachs. _____

4 There are some buildings old. _____

5 The train satation is near the bank. _____

6 There is a interesting market. _____

4 Write about a famous place in your country.

The Burj Al Arab is a famous hotel in Dubai.
There are some expensive restaurants.
There is a beautiful beach near the hotel.
There is a park near the hotel.

→ _____ is a famous _____

→ in _____.

→ There _____

→ _____.

→ There _____

→ _____.

→ There _____

→ _____.

UNIT 8 SPENDING

1 🔊 **8.1** Listen and read. Then trace. Listen again and say.

1 a laptop

2 a video game

3 a T-shirt

4 a newspaper

5 a bank card

6 a watch

7 a smartphone

8 a tablet

2 🔊 **8.2** Read and complete. Then listen and check.

| smartphone | laptop | ~~bank card~~ | T-shirt | tablet |
| video game | newspaper | watch | | |

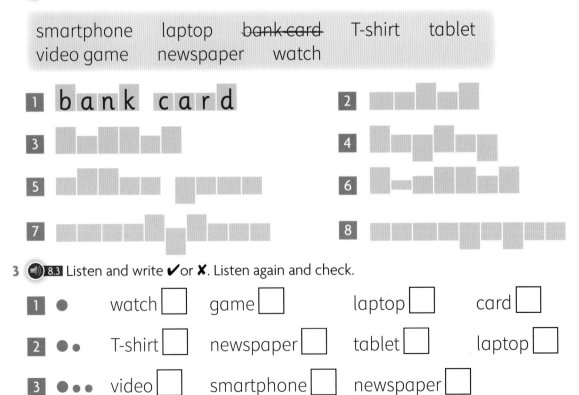

1 **b a n k   c a r d**

2

3

4

5

6

7

8

3 🔊 **8.3** Listen and write ✔ or ✗. Listen again and check.

1 ● watch ☐ game ☐ laptop ☐ card ☐

2 ●● T-shirt ☐ newspaper ☐ tablet ☐ laptop ☐

3 ●●● video ☐ smartphone ☐ newspaper ☐

4 🔊 8.4 Read and write. Then listen and check.

have   ~~T-shirts~~   a lot of

1

How many __T-shirts__
do you _____ ?
I have _____ T-shirts.

you   watch   watches

2

How many _____ do _____ have?

I have one _____ .

do   many   games

3

How _____ video games _____
you have?

I do not have a lot of video _____ .

5 🔊 8.5 Read and write. Then listen and check.

1   How many watches do you have?

   I have two watches _____ .

2   How many tablets do you have?

   I _____ .

3   How many laptops _____ ?

   I have one laptop.

4   _____ ?

   I have a lot of T-shirts.

6 🔊 8.6 Listen and ⟨circle⟩. Then write.

NOTICE ❗

1 I ___**have**___ a lot of bank cards.
(⟨have⟩/ has)

2 I _____ not have a laptop.
(does / do)

3 How many video games does she _____ ?
(has / have)

4 She _____ not have a tablet.
(does / do)

5 He does not _____ a smartphone.
(have / has)

6 How many T-shirts do you _____ ?
(have / has)

NOTICE ❗

How many tablets do you have?

I have two tablets.

I do not have a tablet.

How many watches does she have?

She has three watches.

She does not have a watch.

7 🔊 8.7 Read and correct. Then write **.** or **?** . Listen and check.

1 I do have ⟨not⟩ a watch **.**

2 How many do you T-shirts have

3 How many bank cards do have you

4 She does have not a tablet

8 Writing Challenge Write about your friend.

My friend Suhail

Suhail has two laptops.

He has a lot of T-shirts.

He does not have a watch.

My friend _____

LISTENING AND READING 2

1 🔊 **8.8** Look and match. Then listen.

☐ Monday ☐ S M T W T F S ☐ September ☐ 2017

1 a year **2** a month **3** a day **4** a week

2 🔊 **8.9** Look and trace. Then listen.

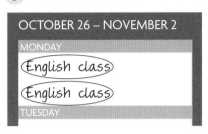

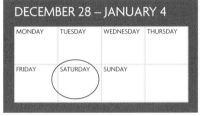

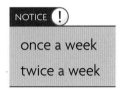

> NOTICE ❗
>
> once a week
>
> twice a week

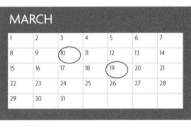

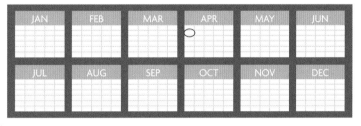

3 🔊 **8.10** Look and complete. Then listen and check.

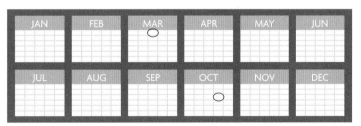

1 once a **d a y**   **2** twice ▢ ▢▢▢▢

3  week   **4** ▢▢▢▢▢ ▢ month

4 🔊 8.11 Listen and say. Then circle *1, 2* or *3*.

| every week | twice a month | once a year | every day |

| 1 ● ●● | 2 ● ●● | 3 ●●● |

NOTICE ❗

I buy a newspaper twice a week.

She buys lunch once a week.

5 Look and read. Write ✔ or ✘.

MON ✘	TUE	WED	THU
FRI	SAT	SUN	

☐

1 I buy a newspaper once a day.

1	2 ✘	3	4	5	6	7
8	9	10	11	12	13	14
15	16	17	18	19	20	21
22	23	24	25	26	27	28
29	30					

☐

2 She buys a video game once a month.

JAN	FEB ✘	MAR	APR	MAY	JUN
JUL	AUG ✘	SEP	OCT	NOV	DEC

☐

3 He buys a mobile phone once a year.

MON ✘	TUE ✘	WED ✘	THU ✘
FRI ✘	SAT ✘	SUN ✘	

☐

4 He buys lunch once a week.

6 🔊 8.12 Listen and write. Then listen and check.

1 Hussain buys a coffee _____ .

2 He buys a newspaper _____ .

3 He buys lunch _____ .

4 He buys a tablet _____ .

7 🔊 8.13 Find the words. Then listen and check.

1 They|buy|anewTVonceayear.

2 Ibuyacoffeeonceaday.

3 Hemeetsfriendstwiceamonth.

4 Sheeatsfishtwiceaweek.

UNLOCK BASIC LITERACY

8 🔊 **8.14** Read and (circle). Then listen and check.

> **1** **once**   He buys a newspaper once a week.
> **2** **twice**   I walk to university twice a week.
> **3** **month**   They travel to different countries once a month.

9 Look. Then cover and complete.

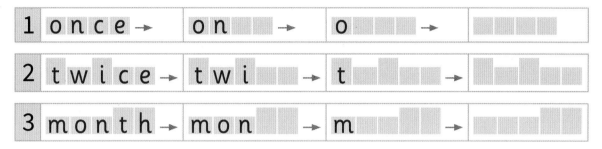

10 🔊 **8.15** Listen and write. Then listen and check.

> once   ~~twice~~   month

> **1** She buys a coffee _____ *twice* _____ a day.
>
> **2** They buy a video game once a _____ .
>
> **3** He reads a newspaper _____ a week.

11 🔊 **8.16** Write the sentences. Then listen and check.

> **1** a smartphone / I / buy / once a year.
>
> _____
>
> **2** twice a month. / He / a video game / buys
>
> _____
>
> **3** buys / a T-shirt / once a month. / She
>
> _____

1 🔊 **8.17** Listen and look. Read and complete. Then write.

> cash   money   card   shoes   ~~shopping~~   clothes

1 go **s h o p p i n g**   _go shopping_

2 spend ▮▮▮▮▮▮   _____

3 buy ▮▮▮▮▮▮▮▮   _____

4 buy ▮▮▮▮   _____

5 pay by ▮▮▮▮▮   _____

6 pay by ▮▮▮▮   _____

2 🔊 **8.18** Look and match. Then listen.

a   b   c

1 on the internet   **2** at the shopping centre   **3** at the market

3 🔊 **8.19** Listen and read. Then trace. Listen again and say.

1

A: → How often do you go shopping
→ at the market?

B: → I go shopping once a week.

2

A: → How often do you buy shoes?

B: → I buy shoes once a month.

3

A: → Where do you buy shoes?

B: → I buy new shoes on the internet.

4

A: → Do you pay by cash?

B: → Yes, I do.

NOTICE ❗

How often do you go shopping?	I go shopping once a day.
Where do you buy new clothes?	I buy new clothes at the market.
Do you pay by cash?	Yes, I do. No, I don't.

---

 4 Writing Challenge Write about your shopping. Answer the questions.

Questions

1 How often do you buy clothes?
I buy clothes once a week.

2 Do you buy clothes at the shopping centre?
Yes, I do.

3 Where do you buy shoes?
I buy shoes on the internet.

1 How often do you buy clothes?
_____
→ _____

2 Do you buy clothes at the shopping centre?
_____
→ _____

3 Where do you buy shoes?
_____
→ _____

SOUND AND SPELLING *ay, a_e, ai*

5 🔊 **8.20** Listen and read. Then trace. Listen again and say.

→ I buy a newspaper once a day.

→ The shop is in the train station.

6 🔊 **8.21** Listen and read. Then trace. Listen again and say.

1	pay	tray	say	play

2	game	face	tape	wave

3	chain	paint	brain	tail

7 🔊 **8.22** Spelling Challenge Look and correct. Then listen and check.

1. daye — I walk to school twice a _____ **day** _____.

2. gaems — He has a lot of video _____.

3. trian — The _____ station is near the shop.

4. paey — They _____ by card.

5. newspaepr — She buys a _____ once a week.

LANGUAGE FOCUS

1 🔊 **8.23** Listen and look. Then read and match.

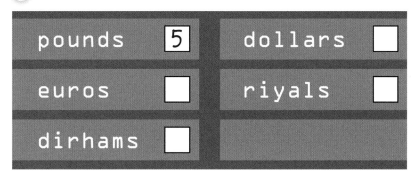

pounds	5	dollars	☐
euros	☐	riyals	☐
dirhams	☐		

1 Saudi Arabia   2 the UAE   3 Europe

4 the USA   5 the UK

2 Look and match.

1 €   2 $ 3 £

☐ dollars   ☐ pounds   ☐ euros

3 🔊 **8.24** Read and trace. Then listen and say.

→ **ten** euros   €10

$100 → **one hundred** dollars

→ **one** thousand dollars $1000

£10,000 → **ten thousand** pounds

→ **one** hundred **thousand** euros €100,000

£100,000,000 → **one** million pounds

4 🔊 **8.25** Read and match. Then listen and check.

471 — four hundred and seventy-one

2,005,000 — two million five thousand

9,633 — nine thousand six hundred and thirty-three

5 🔊 **8.26** Read and complete. Then listen and check.

1 2,950   **t w o**   **t h o u s a n d** ▯▯▯▯

▯▯▯▯▯▯▯ ▯▯▯ ▯▯▯▯

2 6,145   ▯▯ ▯▯▯▯▯▯ ▯▯▯▯ ▯▯▯▯▯ ▯▯▯▯

▯▯▯ ▯▯▯▯▯▯▯▯

3 5,004,000   ▯▯▯ ▯▯▯▯▯▯ ▯▯▯

▯▯▯▯▯▯▯▯

6 Read and match.

1 How much is the video game?

It is 950 dollars.

2 How much is the smartphone?

It is 25 riyals.

> NOTICE ❗
>
> 250   two hundred and fifty
>
> 1,860   one thousand eight hundred and sixty

7 🔊 **8.27** Listen, read and ⬭circle⬭. Listen again and write.

1 How much is the tablet?   50 / ⬭150⬭

It is 150 riyals.

2 How much is the watch?   125 / 225

_____

3 How much is the coffee?   2 / 3

_____

4 How much is the television?   230 / 320

_____

SOUND AND SPELLING *nd, ng*

8 🔊 8.28 Listen and read. Then trace. Listen again and say.

Jules goes shopping once a day.

He buys hundreds of new things twice a week.

He spends thousands of pounds on the internet.

9 🔊 8.29 Listen and read.

		nd	**ng**	
1		ha**nd**	ha**ng**	
2		wi**nd**	wi**ng**	
3		ba**nd**	ba**ng**	

10 🔊 8.30 Look at **9**. Listen and ⌾circle⌾.

LISTENING FOCUS

1 🔊 8.31 Listen and tick ✔.

money ☐   studies at university ☐   family ☐

2 🔊 8.32 Listen, read and (circle). Then listen and check.

1 I buy a newspaper once a **day** / **month**.

2 I think I spend 20 **dirhams** / **riyals** on newspapers once a day.

3 I buy **books** / **newspapers** once a month.

4 I spend 150 dirhams on books once a **year** / **month**.

5 I buy a **smartphone** / **tablet** twice a year.

6 I think I spend 500 dirhams on a smartphone once a **year** / **month**.

7 I pay **by card** / **by cash**.

8 I buy things **at the shopping centre** / **on the internet**.

3 🔊 8.33 Listen and write.

2,500   150   20

1 I spend _____ dirhams on newspapers twice a week.

2 I spend _____ dirhams on books twice a month.

3 I spend _____ dirhams on a smartphone once a year.

⊙ KEY WORDS FOR LITERACY

1 🔊 8.34 Read and (circle). Then listen and check.

1	**by**	She pays by card.
2	**buy**	They buy coffee once a day.
3	**have**	I have a new tablet.
4	**and**	It is six hundred and sixty-two.

2 Look and (circle).

1	**by**	→ buy	→ by	→ buy	→ by	→ be
2	**buy**	→ by	→ (buy)	→ bug	→ bay	→ buy
3	**have**	→ have	→ had	→ have	→ hate	→ have
4	**and**	→ an	→ add	→ and	→ and	→ an

3 Look. Then cover and complete.

1	b y →	b ▢ →	▢ y →	▢ ▢
2	b u y →	b u ▢ →	b ▢ ▢ →	▢ ▢ ▢
3	h a v e →	h a v ▢ →	h ▢ ▢ ▢ →	▢ ▢ ▢ ▢
4	a n d →	a n ▢ →	a ▢ ▢ →	▢ ▢ ▢

4 🔊 8.35 Listen and write. Then listen and check.

1 I _____ a new book twice a week.

2 They pay _____ card twice a day.

3 I _____ a new smartphone.

4 It is three hundred _____ eighty-three.

1 🔊 **8.36** Look and complete. Then listen and say.

shoes   ~~house~~   school   clothes   health

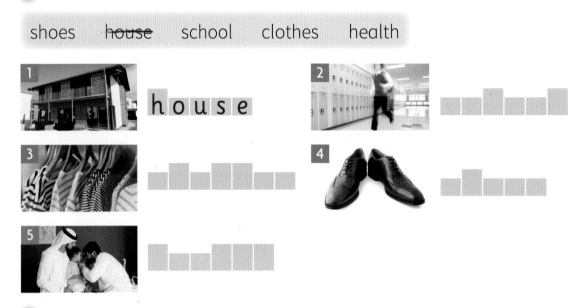

1. h o u s e

2 🔊 **8.37** Look, read and add. Then listen.

The Philippines   Jordan   Brazil

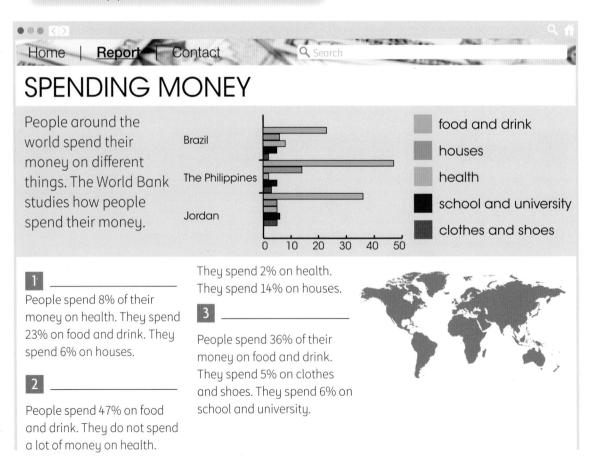

SPENDING MONEY

People around the world spend their money on different things. The World Bank studies how people spend their money.

Legend:
- food and drink
- houses
- health
- school and university
- clothes and shoes

Chart axis: 0 10 20 30 40 50

Countries: Brazil, The Philippines, Jordan

1 _____

People spend 8% of their money on health. They spend 23% on food and drink. They spend 6% on houses.

2 _____

People spend 47% on food and drink. They do not spend a lot of money on health.

They spend 2% on health. They spend 14% on houses.

3 _____

People spend 36% of their money on food and drink. They spend 5% on clothes and shoes. They spend 6% on school and university.

3 🔊 8.37 Look at 2. Read and write. Then listen again and check.

1️⃣ People in Brazil spend ____% every year on health.

2️⃣ In Brazil, people spend 23% of their money on

_____ .

3️⃣ In the Philippines, people spend 2% on

_____ .

4️⃣ People in the Philippines spend 14% on

_____ .

5️⃣ People in Jordan spend ____% on food and drink.

6️⃣ In Jordan, people spend 5% every year on

_____ .

4 Read. Then write about your friend.

Ali

Ali and money

Ali has a lot of video games.

He buys video games once a month.

He spends 50 dirhams on one video game.

He pays by card.

My friend has a lot of _____ .

My friend buys _____

once a _____ .

My friend spends _____ on

_____ .

My friend pays _____ .

UNIT 9 TECHNOLOGY

1 🔊 **9.1** Look and complete. Then listen and check.

> video games   ~~a blog~~   a USB drive   a webinar
> an app   a website   online   GPS

write **a b l o g**

buy ▢▢▢ ▢▢▢

look at ▢▢ ▢▢▢▢▢▢▢

use ▢▢▢

use ▢▢ ▢▢▢▢▢▢▢▢

watch ▢▢ ▢▢▢▢▢▢▢▢

learn English ▢▢▢▢▢▢▢

play ▢▢▢▢▢▢ ▢▢▢▢▢

SOUND AND SPELLING REVIEW

2 🔊 **9.2** Match and write. Listen and check. Then say.

write	~~listen~~	blog	website
app	use	game	webinar

1 fifty _____listen_____

2 bag _____

3 ten _____

4 name _____

5 five _____ _____

6 hot _____

7 June _____

3 🔊 **9.3** Listen and read. Tick ✔.

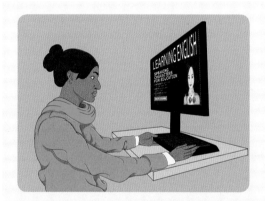

I'm Khadijah. I often play video games. I always learn English online. I sometimes use GPS.

This is my friend, Hana. She usually watches webinars. She never writes blogs.

1 video games   Khadijah ☐   Hana ☐

2 webinars   Khadijah ☐   Hana ☐

3 English online   Khadijah ☐   Hana ☐

4 GPS   Khadijah ☐   Hana ☐

NOTICE ❗

buy an app   buy apps

play a video game

play video games

4 Look and complete.

0% ◄━━━━━━━━━━━━━━━━━━► 100%

never sometimes often usually always

5 🔊 9.4 Read and (circle). Listen and check.

1 **never**   I (never) watch webinars.
2 **sometimes**   I sometimes buy apps.
3 **usually**   I usually learn English online.
4 **often**   I often use GPS.
5 **always**   I always have a USB drive.

6 🔊 9.5 Write the sentences. Then listen and check.

1 watch / I / webinars. / sometimes

I sometimes watch webinars.

2 apps. / usually / buys / He

_____

3 never / a USB drive. / use / I

_____

4 looks at / always / She / websites.

_____

always   never   often   sometimes

I always use GPS. I never use a USB
drive. I often look at English websites.

✏️ 7 Writing Challenge Write about you.

LISTENING AND READING 2

1 🔊 9.6 Look and complete. Then listen and check.

| use | cook | use | take | send | go | ~~use~~ |

1 **u s e** a USB drive

2  ⬜⬜⬜⬜ messages

3  ⬜⬜⬜⬜

4  ⬜⬜ online

5  ⬜⬜⬜⬜ photographs

6  ⬜⬜⬜⬜ the internet

7 ⬜⬜⬜ GPS

2 🔊 9.7 Listen and write. Then listen and say.

| read messages | **3** | cook | ⬜ | take photographs | ⬜ |
| send messages | ⬜ | go online | ⬜ | | |

1 ●   **2** ●●●   **3** ●●●●

3 🔊 **9.8** Listen and read. Then match.

A smart fridge

Malia

I have a smart fridge. It can send messages about old food. It can't cook food.

A smart chair

Jeff

I have a smart chair. It can go online. It can't take photographs.

1 take photographs ✗
3 send messages ✓

2 cook food ✗
4 go online ✓

4 Write.

1 It **can't** use the internet.

It ___cannot___ use the internet .

NOTICE ❗

It can take photographs.

🚫 It can't take photographs.
✏️ It cannot take photographs.

2 It **can't** send messages.

It _____ send messages.

3 It **can't** cook.

It _____ cook.

5 🔊 9.9 Find the words. Then listen and check.

1 Itcansendmessages,butitcannottakephotographs.

2 ItcanplayTV,butitcannotgoonline.

3 Itcannotsendmessages,butitcantakephotographs.

6 🔊 9.10 Look and write. Listen and check.

1 It / but it cannot / can use the internet, / send messages.

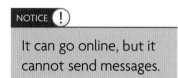

NOTICE ⚠

It can go online, but it cannot send messages.

It can use the internet, but it cannot send messages.

2 can send messages about food, / It / cook. / but it cannot

_____

3 but it cannot / It / can play TV, / go online.

_____

7 Writing Challenge Write about a smart TV.

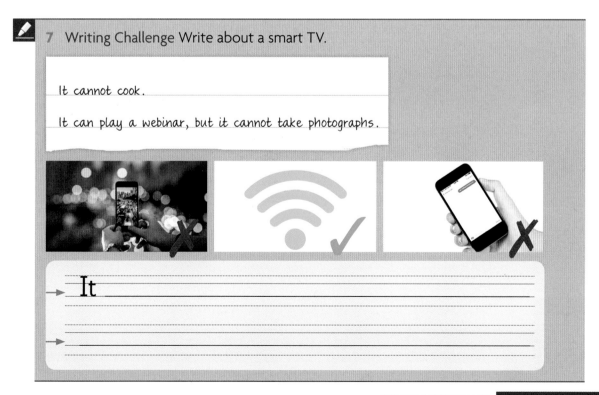

It cannot cook.

It can play a webinar, but it cannot take photographs.

It _____

1 🔊 **9.11** Listen and read. Then trace. Listen again and say.

1	a person	2	a woman
3	a man	4	a girl
5	a boy	6	a child
7	an adult

2 🔊 **9.12** Read and complete. Then listen and check.

women people adults ~~men~~ girls children boys

	🚹	🚺🚹 +
1	a man	m e n
2	a woman	
3	a girl	
4	a boy	
5	a child	
6	an adult	
7	a person	

3 🔊 9.13 Listen and spell.

1 a person ___*people*___   **2** a child _____

3 a man _____   **4** a woman _____

4 🔊 9.14 Listen and read. Then trace. Listen again and say.

MON	TUE	WED	THU	FRI	SAT	SUN

1 week = 7 ~~days~~

01.00	02.00	03.00	04.00	05.00	06.00	07.00	08.00	09.00	10.00	11.00	12.00
13.00	14.00	15.00	16.00	17.00	18.00	19.00	20.00	21.00	22.00	23.00	24.00

1 day = 24 ~~hours~~

 1 hour = 60 ~~minutes~~

 1 minute = 60 ~~seconds~~

 365 days = 1 ~~year~~

5 Read and match.

People and Technology
- **40% of people in the world go online every second.**
- **A lot of children play a new video game every week.**
- **People send 16 million messages every minute.**
- **In the USA, 64% of men and 50% of women use GPS every day.**
- **People buy two hundred and twenty million computers every year.**

NOTICE ❗

40% of adults use the internet **every second**.

People send 16 million messages **every minute**.

A lot of children play video games **every day**.

a   b   c   d   e

1 every second [ ]   **2** every week [ ]

3 every minute [b]   **4** every day [ ]

5 every year [ ]

SOUND AND SPELLING *bl, pl, gl*

6 🔊 **9.15** Listen and read. Then trace. Listen again and say.

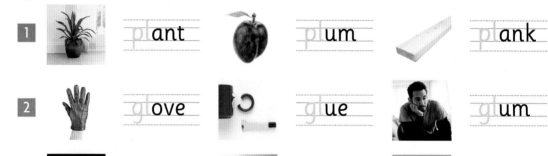

He writes a blog.

They play video games.

She has smart glasses.

7 🔊 **9.16** Listen and read. Then trace. Listen again and say.

1	plant	plum	plank
2	glove	glue	glum
3	black	blank	blue

8 🔊 **9.17** Listen and read.

| 1 | | blue | glue | | 2 | | plank | blank | |
| 3 | | glum | plum | | | | | | |

9 🔊 **9.18** Look at **8**. Listen again and circle.

th' **10** 🔊 **9.19** Spelling Challenge Look and correct. Then listen and check.

1	**palys**	She ___plays___ video games.
2	**galasses**	He has smart _____ .
3	**bolg**	I sometimes write a _____ .

LANGUAGE FOCUS

1 🔊 9.20 Listen and read. Match. Then trace.

a   b   c   d $2000

1	boring	2	interesting
3	expensive	4	great

2 🔊 9.21 Read and match. Then listen and check.

a   b   c

What do you think of my smartwatch?   What do you think of video games?   What do you think of this English website?

1   I think they are boring.   2   I think it is interesting.

3   I think it is very expensive.

3 🔊 9.22 Find the words. Then listen and check.

1   **A:** What|do|youthinkofmylaptop?

    B: Ithinkitisinteresting.

2   **A:** Whatdoyouthinkofsmartwatches?

    B: Ithinktheyareexpensive.

3   **A:** Whatdoyouthinkofthiswebsite?

    B: Ithinkitisgreat.

NOTICE ❗

A: What do you think of my smartwatch?

B: I think it is great.

A: What do you think of video games?

B: I think they are boring.

4 🔊 **9.23** Listen and read. Then write.

~~phone~~   boring   tablet   photographs   video games   TV

1 A: What do you think of this
_____ **phone** _____ ?

B: I think it's _____ .

A: I think so too. It doesn't have
a game.

B: Yes. It can send messages, but it
can't take _____ .

2 A: What do you think of this
_____ ?

B: I think it's good.

A: I disagree. It's expensive, but it
can't play _____ .

B: It has _____ . It's
great!

A: I don't think so.

5 Read **4** again. Then match **1–4** with **a** or **b**.

1 | **a** | I agree.

a 😊

2 | | I don't think so.

3 | | I think so too.

b 😞

4 | | I disagree.

NOTICE ⚠️

🔊 don't   ✏️ do not
🔊 it's   ✏️ it is

6 Write.

1 ✔ I think _____ **it** _____
_____ good.

2 ✘ I _____ _____
think so.

SOUND AND SPELLING *dge*, *tch*

7 🔊 **9.24** Listen and read. Then trace. Listen again and say.

A smart fri<u>dge</u> uses the internet.

Some people wa<u>tch</u> TV on smartphones.

8 🔊 **9.25** Listen and read. Then trace. Listen again and say.

	dge		tch	
1		bri<u>dge</u>	ca<u>tch</u>	
2		he<u>dge</u>	ma<u>tch</u>	
3		ju<u>dge</u>	sti<u>tch</u>	

9 🔊 **9.26** Listen and read. Write. Then say.

1

We need to ca **t c h** the bus to the
ma __ __ __ .

2

The he __ __ __ stops at the bri __ __ __ .

3

The ju __ __ __ needs a sti __ __ __ in his coat .

10 🔊 **9.27** Spelling Challenge Look and correct. Then listen and check.

1 frigde _____   2 wacth _____

LISTENING FOCUS

1 🔊 **9.28** Listen and complete the sentence.

It is about
1 tablets.
2 smartphones.
3 video games.
4 smartwatches.

2 🔊 **9.29** Listen and tick ✔.

1 Students learn English online on a smartphone. Badar ☐ Saud ☐

2 Some students play games on smartphones. Badar ☐ Saud ☐

3 You don't listen in class with smartphones. Badar ☐ Saud ☐

4 Some students write messages on a smartphone. Badar ☐ Saud ☐

3 🔊 **9.29** Listen again and circle.

1 I agree. Teacher / (Badar) / Saud

2 I don't think so. Teacher / Badar / Saud

3 I disagree. Teacher / Badar / Saud

4 I think so too. Teacher / Badar / Saud

4 🔊 **9.30** Listen and circle.

1 I think they are (**very good**) / **interesting**.

2 I think smartphones are **boring** / **bad** for students.

3 It's **expensive** / **difficult** for students.

4 It's **interesting** / **boring**.

5 A lot of things are **great** / **good**.

⊙ KEY WORDS FOR LITERACY

1 🔊 9.31 Read and circle. Then listen and check.

1	**can**	It can go online.
2	**never**	Some men and women never play video games.
3	**often**	This woman often writes a blog.
4	**always**	I always learn English online.

2 Look and circle.

1	**can**	→	(can)	→	man	→	can't	→	can
2	**never**	→	fever	→	never	→	fewer	→	never
3	**often**	→	after	→	offer	→	often	→	often
4	**always**	→	airways	→	always	→	always	→	away

3 Look. Then cover and complete.

| 1 | c a n → | c a ◻ → | ◻◻◻ → | ◻◻◻◻ |

| 2 | n e v e r → | n e v ◻ → | n e ◻◻◻ → | ◻◻◻◻◻ |

| 3 | o f t e n → | o f t ◻ → | o f ◻◻◻ → | ◻◻◻◻ |

| 4 | a l w a y s → | a l w a ◻ → |
| | a l w ◻◻ → | ◻◻◻◻◻ |

4 🔊 9.32 Listen and write. Then listen and check.

| and women | sister often | it can | always listen |

1 My _____ plays video games.

2 Some men _____ use the internet.

3 We _____ in class.

4 It's expensive, but _____ take photographs.

1 🔊 **9.33** Look, read and (circle). Then listen.

--- **People and smartphones** ---

1 Adults / Children /(Smartphones)

A lot of people around the world have smartphones. In the UK, 70% of people have smartphones. People spend 2 hours online every day on their smartphones. People only spend 1 hour online every day on their computers. People do a lot of different things on a smartphone. They watch TV and take photographs. Adults and young people use smartphones for different things.

2 Adults / Children / Smartphones

65% of adults have a smartphone. 55% of adults take photographs with smartphones. 30% of adults use their phones every five minutes. 18% watch TV on their smartphones.

3 Adults / Children / Smartphones

90% of young people have smartphones. 90% of young people take photographs with smartphones. 45% check their phones every five minutes. 42% watch TV on their smartphones.

2 Look at **1**. Read and write.

1 People spend two hours every _____ on their smartphones.

2 Adults and young people _____ smartphones for different things.

3 65% of adults have a _____ .

4 Not a lot of adults _____ TV on their smartphones.

5 A lot of young people take _____ with smartphones.

6 45% of young people use their smartphones _____ five minutes.

3 Read and add **.** and **,** .

> **1** A lot of people go online on their smartphones __ but not a lot of adults watch TV __

> **2** Some people look at websites and they write blogs __

4 Read and add *and* or *but*. Write the sentences.

> **1** It can send messages. It can have a USB drive.
>
> _____
>
> **2** It can go online. It cannot cook.
>
> _____

5 Write about your tablet or smartphone.

My tablet

every day

✔ go online

✗ take photographs

I use my tablet every day.
It can go online.
It can't take photographs.

My _____

every _____

✔ _____

✗ _____

→ I _____

→ _____

→ _____

UNIT 10 FREE TIME AND FASHION

LISTENING AND READING 1

1 🔊 **10.1** Listen and read. Then trace. Match.

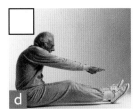

1 go for a walk

2 bake cakes

3 have a picnic

4 do exercise

5 talk on the phone

6 go to the park

7 visit friends and family

8 go shopping

2 🔊 **10.2** Look at **1** and match. Then listen and check.

a ●● ☐

b ●●● ☐

c ●●●● ☐

d ●●●●● ☐

e ●●●●●●● ☐

f ●●●● ☐ ☐ ☐

3 🔊 **10.3** Read and tick ✔. Then listen.

Home | Questions | Writing | About | Email

University life – a student blog

What do you do in your free time?

In my free time, I do exercise at home. I also talk on the phone. I visit friends and family on Friday. We go to the park. We also go for a walk.

1 ☐ do exercise at home   **2** ☐ have a picnic

3 ☐ talk on the phone   **4** ☐ visit friends and family

5 ☐ bake cakes   **6** ☐ go to the park

7 ☐ go shopping   **8** ☐ go for a walk

4 🔊 **10.4** Read and circle. Then listen and check.

1 **also**   She also does exercise at home.

2 **walk**   He goes for a walk.

3 **talk**   I often talk on the phone.

5 Look and circle.

1 **also**	→ all	→ (also)	→ so	→ also	→ and
2 **walk**	→ walk	→ wall	→ what	→ walk	→ walk
3 **talk**	→ tall	→ talk	→ that	→ tall	→ talk

6 🔊 **10.5** Read and circle. Correct. Then listen and check.

1 I talk (with) the phone every day. _____*on*_____

2 I go to a walk. _____

3 I usually do exercise for home. _____

4 I also go on the park. _____

5 I often talk at the phone. _____

NOTICE ❗
go for a walk
talk on the phone
go to the park
do exercise at home

7 🔊 **10.6** Write the sentences. Then listen and check.

1 cakes. / I / bake / also

I also bake cakes.

NOTICE ❗

I do exercise at home and I talk on the phone.

= I do exercise at home. I **also** talk on the phone.

2 also / shopping. / I / go

_____

3 a picnic. / have / I / also

_____

4 for a walk. / also / go / I

_____

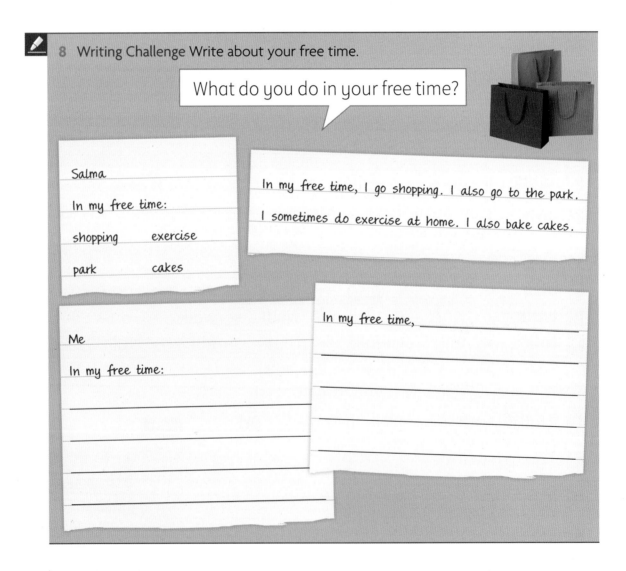

8 Writing Challenge Write about your free time.

What do you do in your free time?

Salma

In my free time:

shopping   exercise

park   cakes

In my free time, I go shopping. I also go to the park.
I sometimes do exercise at home. I also bake cakes.

Me

In my free time:

_____

_____

_____

In my free time, _____

_____

_____

_____

LISTENING AND READING 2

1 🔊 10.7 Listen and read. Then trace. Listen again and say.

 1 **wait**

 2 *sleep*

 3 *draw*

 4 *chat online*

2 🔊 10.8 Look and complete. Then listen and check.

take   ~~drive~~   write   buy   go   travel   watch   learn

1 **d r i v e** a car

2 ☐☐ shopping

3 ☐☐☐ photographs

4 ☐☐☐☐ TV

5 ☐☐☐☐ a blog

6 ☐☐☐ new languages

7 ☐☐☐☐ to different countries

8 ☐☐☐ new clothes

SOUND AND SPELLING REVIEW

3 🔊 10.9 Match and write. Listen and check. Then say.

drive   go   take   write   ~~languages~~   travel

1 bag   _languages_   _____

2 bake _____

3 nine _____   _____

4 no   _____

4 🔊 **10.10** Listen and read. Write **T** (Tariq) or **O** (Omar).

ALI: Hi Tariq! I'm Ali from the student newspaper. What do you like doing in your free time?

TARIQ: In my free time, I like watching TV on my smartphone. I also like drawing. I don't like going shopping.

ALI: Thank you. And your brother, Omar? What does he like doing?

TARIQ: He likes learning new languages and he likes cooking. But he doesn't like baking cakes.

1 ✓ 2 ✓ 3 ✓ 4 ✗ 5 6 ✓

SOUND AND SPELLING -ing

5 Read. Then trace and write.

watch + -ing = _watching_

1 buy _buying_

2 wait _____

3 draw _____

bake + -ing = bak~~e~~ing = _baking_

4 write _____   5 drive _____

6 take _____

chat + ing = chat + **t** + -ing = _chatting_

7 travel _____

6 Look and write.

I _____*like*_____ _____*writing*_____
my blog.

She _____ _____ to
different countries.

I _____ _____
_____ with friends.

He _____ _____
_____ photographs.

7 Writing Challenge Write about your friend.

My friend Shadi

✔ chat with friends   ✔ sleep   ✗ wait   ✗ talk

Shadi likes chatting with friends. He also likes sleeping.

He does not like waiting. He does not like talking on the phone.

My friend _____

✔ _____   ✔ _____

✗ _____   ✗ _____

1 🔊 **10.11** Listen and read. Then trace and write. Listen again and say.

1	a coat
2	a shirt
3	a jacket
4	a dress
5	a hat
6	a scarf
7	trousers
8	shoes

2 🔊 **10.12** Look and complete. Listen and check. Then trace.

T-shirt   shoes   ~~coat~~   scarf   jeans

1   wear a **c o a t** and a ☐☐☐☐☐☐

2   wear a ☐☐☐☐☐☐ and
☐☐☐☐☐

3   wear ☐☐☐☐

3 🔊 **10.13** Listen and read. Then write.

What's this?

A: This is a coat from India.

B: It's beautiful.

A: Thank you. Look. This is an expensive scarf from Turkey. I like wearing clothes from Turkey.

B: What are these?

A: These are my shoes. They are from the USA, but they are old.

~~India~~   the USA   expensive   Turkey   old   beautiful

1 The coat is from ___India___ . It is _____ .

2 The scarf is from _____ . It is _____ .

3 The shoes are from _____ .

They are _____ .

> NOTICE ❗
>
> This is a coat.
> These are my shoes.

4 🔊 **10.14** Read and <u>underline</u>. Listen and check. Then trace.

1 ~~This is~~ / ~~These are~~ my new shoes.

2 ~~This is~~ / ~~These are~~ my dress.

3 ~~This is~~ / ~~These are~~ a hat from India.

4 ~~This is~~ / ~~These are~~ his shoes.

5 ~~This is~~ / ~~These are~~ beautiful trousers.

6 ~~This is~~ / ~~These are~~ my new clothes.

SOUND AND SPELLING REVIEW

5 🔊 **10.15** Listen and read. Then trace. Listen again and say.

1 bread   friend   group   2 photograph   food

3 blog   glasses   play   4 train   station   street

5 chat   think   shop   6 airport   park   bank   first

6 🔊 **10.16** Listen and read. Listen and write. Then say.

1 The **t r** ousers are from __ __ ance. The __ __ ess and
   __ __ asses are from __ __ eece.

2 They live near the __ __ ops and the airpo __ __ . I live
   near the pa __ __ , ba __ __ and the __ __ ation.

3 He wa __ __ __ es TV and __ __ ays video games.
   He doesn't take __ __ otographs.

---

th

7 🔊 **10.17** Spelling Challenge Look and correct. Then listen and check.

1 wacth   _watch_   2 sutdent   _____

3 dirink   _____   4 lunech   _____

LANGUAGE FOCUS

1 🔊 10.18 Listen and read. Then trace. Listen again and say.

1 red

2 blue

3 yellow

4 green

5 black

6 white

> NOTICE !
>
> These are red trousers.
> This is a yellow hat.

2 🔊 10.19 Read and match. Then listen and check.

 a
 b
 c
 d
 e
 f 1

1 These are new **white** shirts. 2 These are **black** shoes.

3 These are **red** trousers. 4 This is a beautiful **green** dress.

5 This is a great **blue** T-shirt. 6 This is a **yellow** hat.

SOUND AND SPELLING REVIEW

> NOTICE !
>
> a green beautiful dress
> a beautiful green dress

3 🔊 10.20 Match and write. Then listen and check.

1 thr**ee** _____green_____

2 b**a**g _____

3 n**i**n**e** _____

4 t**e**n _____ _____

red   white   ~~green~~
black   yellow

4 Read and tick ✔.

 This is my brother's jacket. My brother's jacket is blue. It is old, but he likes wearing it.

 These are Julia's shoes. Julia's shoes are white and they are from the UK. They are also new.

1 My brother's jacket is

black ☐   blue ☐   old ☐   cold ☐

2 Julia's shoes are

white ☐   wet ☐   from the UK ☐   from the USA ☐

5 🔊 **10.21** Read and add **'s** . Then listen and check.

1 This is Janet**'s** hat.

2 These are Simon__ trousers.

3 My father__ coat is green.

4 Laila__ scarf is yellow.

> **NOTICE** ❗
>
> This is my brother's jacket.
> Julia's shoes are white.

6 🔊 **10.22** Read and add **and**, **but** or **also**. Then listen and check.

1 Alia's shoes are green^they are expensive. _____

2 I like wearing black clothes. I^like wearing red clothes.

_____

3 This is Amna's scarf. It is new,^she does not like wearing it.

_____

4 My sister's coat is black^it is from the UK. _____

SOUND AND SPELLING REVIEW

7 🔊 10.23 Listen and read. Then trace. Listen again and say.

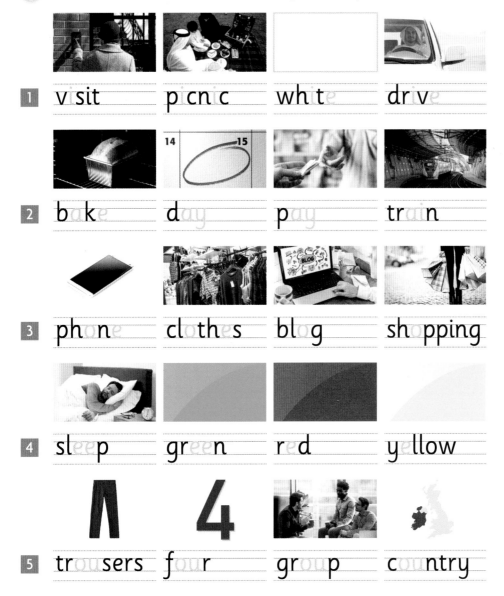

1 | visit | picnic | white | drive

2 | bake | day | pay | train

3 | phone | clothes | blog | shopping

4 | sleep | green | red | yellow

5 | trousers | four | group | country

8 🔊 10.24 Listen and read. Listen and write. Then say.

1   He __ xercises at h __ m __ . He also goes sh __ pping and ch __ ts on the ph __ n __ .

2   She wr __ t __ s a bl __ g about her c __ __ ntry.

3   I l __ k __ th __ s __ gr __ __ n tr __ __ sers.

LISTENING FOCUS

1 🔊 **10.25** Listen and tick ✔. What is this about?

| 1 | Mr Raman's favourite food | ☐ | 2 | Mr Raman's city | ☐ |

| 3 | Mr Raman's clothes | ☐ | 4 | Mr Raman's job | ☐ |

| 5 | Mr Raman's free time | ☐ |

2 🔊 **10.26** Listen and number.

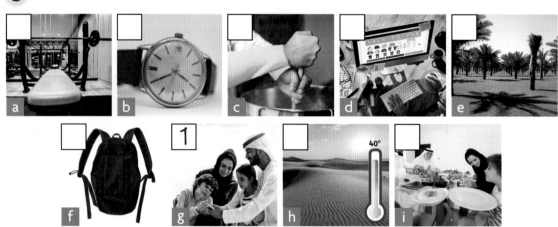

3 🔊 **10.26** Listen again and circle.

1 In the evening, Mr Raman has dinner with his **friends** / **family**.

2 Mr Raman likes doing exercise on **Saturday** / **Sunday**.

3 It is very **hot** / **cold** in Mr Raman's country.

4 Mr Raman exercises at home in **summer** / **winter**.

5 Mr Raman **always** / **sometimes** wears his watch.

6 Mr Raman wears his **grandfather's** / **father's** watch.

7 Mr Raman's brother **doesn't like** / **likes** the bag.

8 Mr Raman's brother doesn't like **black** / **blue**.

⊙ KEY WORDS FOR LITERACY

1 🔊 10.27 Read and (circle). Then listen and check.

1	**this**	This is my friend.
2	**these**	What are these?
3	**they**	They are very expensive.
4	**their**	The students like their class.

2 Look and (circle).

1	**this**	→ (this)	→ thin	→ this	→ these	→ this
2	**these**	→ there	→ these	→ these	→ them	→ there
3	**they**	→ them	→ they	→ the	→ they	→ them
4	**their**	→ their	→ there	→ their	→ this	→ their

3 Look. Then cover and complete.

1	t h i s →	t h i →	t h →	
2	t h e s e →	t h e →	t h →	
3	t h e y →	t h e →	t h →	
4	t h e i r →	t h e →	t h →	

4 🔊 10.28 Listen and write. Then listen and check.

1 _____ trousers are from France.

2 _____ are from Mexico.

3 The students have _____ lunch.

4 _____ jacket is from the USA.

1 (🔊) **10.29** Look and match. Read and check. Then listen.

Abdul ☐ ☐ ☐   Miriam ☐ ☐ ☐

1 London   **2** Riyadh   **3** speak French
4 bake   **5** have a picnic   **6** go shopping

● ● ● ‹ ›   🔍 🏠

Home | Photographs | Contact   🔍 Search

Winter at university in different countries

It is winter. Students have a lot of free time. Abdul is in Riyadh. Miriam is in London. They talk about what they do in winter.

Abdul: In winter, I visit friends and family. I do not like watching TV, but I like learning new languages. I speak English and French. I also like travelling. I like going to the park and having a picnic. My mother's picnics are very good. It is not cold, so I usually wear a T-shirt and trousers. This is my new T-shirt. It is green and it is from the UAE.

Miriam: I like going shopping. It is cold. I like wearing a thick coat and winter shoes. This is my beautiful new coat. It is blue and it is from Spain. I like chatting with friends and watching TV. I like baking cakes, but I do not like cooking dinner.

What do you like doing in winter?
Comments

---

2 Look at **1**. Read and write ✔ or ✘.

1 Abdul likes watching TV.   ✘

2 Abdul likes going to the park. ☐

3 Abdul wears a T-shirt and trousers. ☐

4 Abdul's T-shirt is blue. ☐

5 Miriam likes going shopping. ☐

6 Miriam's coat is from the UK. ☐

7 Miriam likes cooking dinner. ☐

3 Look at the survey. Read and complete the email.

Hi,

These are my answers to the survey.

1 In my free time, I like talking on the

_____ . I also like doing

_____ at home, but I do

not like _____ TV.

2 I like wearing a dress and a

_____ . I do not like

wearing my _____ clothes.

Regards,

Hessa

Free time survey

Your name: Hessa

Q1 What do you like doing in your free time?

✔ _talk on the phone, do exercise_

✘ _watch TV_

Q2 What clothes do you like wearing?

✔ _dress, scarf_

✘ _my sister's clothes_

---

4 Write about your free time.

● ● ●

To: freetime@university.ac.ae

Subject: Free time survey

Reply   Forward

Hi,

These are my answers to the survey.

_____

_____

_____

_____

_____

_____

Regards,

_____

Free time survey

Your name:

_____

Q1 What do you like doing in your free time?

✔ _____

✘ _____

Q2 What clothes do you like wearing?

✔ _____

✘ _____

AUDIO SCRIPTS

STARTER UNIT

🔊 0.1

A: Hello. I'm Ali.

B: Hello. I'm James.

C: Hello. I'm Rashid.

D: Hello. I'm Bader.

E: Hello. I'm Hussain.

F: Hello. I'm Tom.

G: Hello. I'm Younis.

🔊 0.2

A: Hello. I'm Mr Humaid.

B: Hello. I'm Mrs Scott.

🔊 0.11

1   Look and listen.

2   Read and listen.

3   Point and say.

4   Listen and write.

🔊 0.25

k, m, a, p, c, s, d, b, e, l, n, o, v, u, z, t, f, j, g, h, i, q, r, x, w, y

UNIT 1

🔊 1.6

1   **Sami:** I'm Sami.
    A: How do you spell that?
    Sami: S – a – m – i.

2   **Ameena:** My name's Ameena.
    B: How do you spell that?
    Ameena: A – m – double e – n – a.

3   **Qassim:** I'm Qassim.
    A: How do you spell that?
    Qassim: Q – a – double s – i – m.

4   **Rosa:** My name's Rosa.
    B: How do you spell that?
    Rosa: R – o – s – a.

🔊 1.10

1   **A:** Hi, Mehmet. What's your number?
    Mehmet: It's 039 282 9460.

2   **A:** Hi, Abdul Aziz. What's your number?
    Abdul Aziz: It's 0181 285 2865.

3   **B:** Hi, Fatima. What's your number?
    Fatima: It's 07706 468 926.

4   **B:** Hi, Latifa. What's your number?
    Latifa: It's 01253 805 257.

🔊 1.28

Student: Hello.

Librarian: Hi.

Student: Can I have a library card, please?

Librarian: What's your first name?

Student: Paddy.

Librarian: How do you spell that?

Student: P – a – d – d – y.

Librarian: What's your family name?

Student: Bannock.

Librarian: Where are you from?

Student: I'm from the UK.

Librarian: What's your phone number?

Student: 443 218.

Librarian: Please sign here.

Student: Can I have a pen, please?

Librarian: Yes, here you are.

UNIT 2

🔊 2.15

seven seven I have seven bags.
Mexico Mexico He's from Mexico.

UNIT 4

🔊 4.26

Asad: Hello, my name is Asad. I'm from Jeddah. Jeddah is a city in Saudi Arabia. This is Jeddah. This is the desert. It's big and hot. This is the beach. It's beautiful and clean. This is the university. It's new. It's not old.

UNIT 5

🔊 5.3

a A: This is Abdulla.
  B: Is he a photographer?
  A: No, he isn't. He's a pilot.

b A: This is Ronesh.
  B: Is he a dentist?
  A: Yes, he is.

c C: This is Sally.
  D: Is she a police officer?
  C: No, she isn't. She's a bank manager.

🔊 5.8

Sam: Hi. I'm Sam. I work at a bank. I start work at eight-thirty. I finish work at five-thirty. I meet friends at six o'clock.

Ali: Hi. I'm Ali. I study at university. I start classes at nine o'clock. I go to the library at two o'clock. I go home at five o'clock.

🔊 5.11

Ross: My name is Ross. I am a photographer. I take photographs. I meet people in the city.

A: They work in the city. They write emails. They read emails.

B: We are pilots. We travel to different countries. We help people.

🔊 5.25

A: Asma is from the UAE. She is a businesswoman. She travels to different countries. She starts work at eight o'clock.

B: Peter is from the UK. He is a police officer. He works at night. He helps people.

C: Metin and Ahmet are from Turkey. They meet interesting people. They are teachers. They finish classes at two-thirty.

UNIT 6

🔊 6.5

Huda: My name is Huda. I eat fish. I don't drink coffee.

Tariq: My name is Tariq. I eat bread. I don't eat meat.

Natasha: My name is Natasha. I drink green tea. I don't drink juice.

🔊 6.27

Ahmad: My name is Ahmad. Here are the results of my student survey. Number 1 – what do students eat and drink? A lot of students drink coffee with milk. Some students eat fruit and vegetables. Not a lot of students eat red meat. Number 2 – what do students do? A lot of students go to bed late. Some students get up early. Not a lot of students walk to university.

🔊 6.28

Fauzia: My name is Fauzia. Here are the results of my student survey. Number 1 – what do students eat and drink? Not a lot of students drink green tea. Some students eat bread and rice. A lot of students drink juice. Number 2 – what do students do? A lot of students work in the library. Not a lot of students have dinner at university. Some students go to bed early.

UNIT 7

🔊 7.29

1 Dubai Mall

A: This is Dubai Mall. It's a shopping centre in Dubai. It's big and new. There are a lot of shops with cameras, computers, bags and mobile phones. There are a lot of restaurants from different countries. Some restaurants are cheap. There is a tall building.

2 Tsukiji Fish Market

B: This is Tsukiji Fish Market. It's a famous fish market in Tokyo. It starts at 5 o'clock in the morning. There are a lot of small shops. There are some restaurants. A lot of people eat fish in the restaurants. Some people drink green tea. The market is busy. It's a great place.

UNIT 8

🔊 8.31 🔊 8.32

A: I have eight questions, Mr Wells.

Mr Wells: OK. Go ahead.

A: 1 How often do you buy newspapers?

Mr Wells: I buy a newspaper once a day.

A: 2 How much money do you spend on newspapers?

Mr Wells: I think I spend 20 dirhams on newspapers once a day. 🔊 8.32

A: 3 How often do you buy books?

Mr Wells: I buy books once a month.

A: 4 How much money do you spend on books?

Mr Wells: I spend 150 dirhams on books once a month.

A: 5 How often do you buy a smartphone?

Mr Wells: I buy a smartphone twice a year.

A: 6 How much money do you spend on smartphones?

Mr Wells: I think I spend 500 dirhams on a smartphone once a month.

A: 7 Do you pay by card?

Mr Wells: Yes, I do.

A: 8 Do you buy things on the internet?

Mr Wells: No, I don't. I buy things at the shopping centre.

A: Thank you, Mr Wells.

UNIT 9

 9.14

One week is 7 days.
One day is 24 hours.
One hour is 60 minutes.
One minute is 60 seconds.
365 days is one year.

 9.28 🔊 9.29

Teacher: The topic for the Group Talk this week is technology. The title is: Smartphones can help students to learn English. So, everyone, what do you think? Do you agree? Do you disagree? Badar, what about you?

Badar: I agree. Smartphones can help you to learn English. Students go online and you you look at English websites. I think they are very good.

Saud: I don't think so. 🔊 9.29

Teacher: So what do you think, Saud?

Saud: I disagree. I think smartphones are bad for students. Some students go online and play games. It is difficult for students. We need to listen to the teacher. You don't listen when you play games on your phone.

Teacher: That's interesting. Badar, what do you think?

Badar: A lot of things are great. Some students write messages in English. They look at websites in English.

Teacher: I think so too. Good ideas, Badar.

UNIT 10

🔊 10.25 🔊 10.26

A: Excuse me, Mr Raman. I have some questions for a survey. Can you answer them?

Mr Raman: Yes, of course.

A: So, what do you like doing in the evening?

Mr Raman: I like chatting with my family and I like cooking. I …  10.26 I … usually have dinner with my family.

A: Number 2. What do you like doing on Saturday?

Mr Raman: Well, I like doing exercise, but it is very hot in this country. In summer, I exercise at home. In winter, I also like going to the park.

A: Number 3. What do you like wearing to exercise?

Mr Raman: I like wearing sports shoes and T-shirts. I usually shop online. I always wear this watch. It is my father's watch. It is very old. And this is my brother's bag. I like it, but he doesn't like it. He doesn't like blue.

ACKNOWLEDGEMENTS

Author acknowledgements

Emma and Gary Pathare would like to thank those students of Dubai Men's and Women's Colleges who they worked with during the time their interest in and knowledge of L2 literacy developed. They would also like to thank their children for providing contrasting models in the form of L1 literacy development.

Publisher acknowledgments

The publishers are extremely grateful to the following people for reviewing this course during its development. The course had benefited hugely from your insightful comments and feedback.

Ashwaq Al-Jahlan, Princess Noura University, Saudi Arabia; Peggy Alptekin; Dr. Wafa Aws, Dar Al Uloom, Saudi Arabia; Anil Bayir, Izmir University, Turkey; Patrick Boylan, King Abdulaziz University, Saudi Arabia; Pauline Chahine, Qatar Armed Forces, Qatar; Esengul Hademir, Atilim University, Turkey; Dr Anwar Jamal, Kuwait University, Kuwait; Megan Putney, Dhofar University, Oman; Tracy Quayat, Princess Noura Univeristy, Saudi Arabia; Katherine Rick, Lincoln College, Saudi Arabia; Hussein Saeed, Jubail Industrial College, Saudi Arabia

The authors and publishers acknowledge the following sources of copyright material and are grateful for the permissions granted. While every effort has been made, it has not always been possible to identify the sources of all the material used, or to trace all copyright holders. If any omissions are brought to our notice, we will be happy to include the appropriate acknowledgements on reprinting and in the next update to the digital edition, as applicable.

Key: T = Top, L = Left, R = Right, TL = Top Left, TC = Top Centre, TR = Top Right, TCL = Top Centre Left, TCR = Top Centre Right, C = Centre, CL = Centre Left, CR = Centre Right, BL = Below Left, BR = Below Right, B = Below, BC = Below Centre, BCL = Below Centre Left, BCR = Below Centre Right, BG = Background.

p. 11 (T), p. 47 (CL), p. 126 (photo 2): Caiaimage/Robert Daly/OJO+/Getty Images; p. 11 (BL): Zurijeta/iStock/Getty Images Plus/Getty Images; p. 11 (BR): Klaus Vedfelt/Taxi/Getty Images; p. 15 (locker): American Images Inc/Photodisc/Getty Images; p. 15 (door): Luis Alvarenga/EyeEm/Getty Images; p. 15 (t-shirt): karammiri/iStock/Getty Images Plus/Getty Images; p. 15 (arrow): Greg Pease/Stone/Getty Images; p. 15 (fifteen): ermingut/iStock/Getty Images Plus/Getty Images; p. 15 (car), p. 58 (car): Heritage Images/Hulton Archive/Getty Images; p. 16 (listening): se_media/iStock/Getty Images Plus/Getty Images; p. 16 (speaking): Adrianko/Cultura/Getty Images; p. 16 (reading), p. 60 (teacher): Gallo Images/Getty Images; p. 16 (writing): psphotograph/iStock/Getty Images Plus/Getty Images; p. 16 (eyes): wickedpix/iStock/Getty Images Plus/Getty Images; p. 16 (pointing): Mixmike/E+/Getty Images; p. 16 (BL): Hero Images/DigitalVision/Getty Images; p. 16 (BCL): Simon Winnall/Cultura/Getty Images; p. 16 (BCR): annebaek/iStock/Getty Images Plus/Getty Images; p. 16 (BR), p. 49 (CL), p. 86 (T), p. 113 (photo 2, photo 5), p. 119 (tires), p. 125, p. 133 (photo a): Westend61/Getty Images; p. 21 (exit): webphotographeer/E+/Getty Images; p. 21 (go): David Crunelle/EyeEm/Getty Images; p. 21 (stop): Chris Cheadle/All Canada Photos/Getty Images; p. 21 (login): FaysalAhmedFarhan/iStock/Getty Images Plus/Getty Images; p. 21 (Saudi Arabian flag): republica/iStock/Getty Images Plus/Getty Images; p. 21 (UAE flag): Zloyel/iStock/Getty Images Plus/Getty Images; p. 21 (computer): sweetym/E+/Getty Images; p. 21 (UK flag): mills21/iStock/Getty Images Plus/Getty Images; p. 21 (a CD): kaczka/E+/Getty Images; p. 21 (car), p. 84 (TR), p. 153 (smartphone), p. 162 (CL), p. 169 (smart fridge): Bloomberg/Getty Images; p. 21 (ATM): JazzIRT/E+/Getty Images; p. 27 (bus), p. 28 (bus), p. 29 (bus): Charles Bowman/Photolibrary/Getty Images; p. 27 (coffee), p. 29 (coffee): ALEAIMAGE/E+/Getty Images; p. 27 (doctor): fakezzz/iStock/Getty Images Plus/Getty Images; p. 27 (gas), p. 28 (gas), p. 29 (gas): Tatabrada/iStock/Getty Images Plus/Getty Images; p. 27 (meeting), p. 28 (meeting), p. 29 (meeting): Caiaimage/Paul Bradbury/Riser/Getty Images; p. 27 (jeans), p. 28 (jeans), p. 180 (trousers): Jitalia17/E+/Getty Images; p. 27 (weight), p. 28 (weight): Caspar Benson/Getty Images; p. 27 (lemon), p. 28 (lemon), p. 29 (lemon): Phillip Hayson/Photolibrary/Getty Images; p. 27 (texting): Jeff Metzger/Hemera/Getty Images Plus/Getty Images; p. 27 (tree), p. 28 (tree), p. 29 (tree): John Harper/Photolibrary/Getty Images; p. 27 (queen), p. 28 (queen), p. 38 (push): AFP/Getty Images; p. 27 (radio), p. 28 (radio): PeopleImages/iStock/Getty Images Plus/Getty Images; p. 27 (salad), p. 28 (salad), p. 110 (photo 2): Andrew Unangst/Photographer's Choice/Getty Images; p. 27 (video), p. 28 (video), p. 29 (video): YasnaTen/iStock/Getty Images Plus/Getty Images; p. 27 (Wi-Fi), p. 28 (Wi-Fi), p. 29 (Wi-Fi): madebymarco/iStock/Getty Images Plus/Getty Images; p. 27 (taxi): Eric Van Den Brulle/The Image Bank/Getty Images; p. 27 (yacht): laughingmango/E+/Getty Images; p. 30 (photo 1), p. 33 (CL), p. 49 (sisters), p. 105 (cycling):

Patrick Eckersley/arabianEye/Getty Images; p. 30 (photo 2), p. 31 (photo 4.1, photo 4.2), p. 34 (BL), p. 46 (mother), p. 48 (CR), p. 56 (Omar), p. 74, p. 103 (CL), p. 129 (CL), p. 164 (photo 2), p. 174 (photo b), p. 177 (photo 2, photo 8), p. 185 (picnic): Celia Peterson/arabianEye/Getty Images; p. 30 (photo 3): Ariel Skelley/Blend Images/Getty Images; p. 30 (photo 4), p. 44 (photo b): Eugenio Marongiu/Cultura/Getty Images; p. 30 (photo 5), p. 46 (Rami), p. 57 (boy), p. 102 (watch), p. 164 (photo 5), p. 182 (two friends): Image Source/Getty Images; p. 31 (photo 4.3), p. 56 (Taleb), p. 119 (fine): Juanmonino/E+/Getty Images; p. 31 (photo 5.1): Nick Daly/Iconica/Getty Images; p. 31 (photo 5.2), p. 149 (photo 4): Juanmonino/iStock/Getty Images Plus/Getty Images; p. 32 (photo 1), p. 50 (T), p. 97 (photo b): monkeybusinessimages/iStock/Getty Images Plus/Getty Images; p. 32 (photo 2, B), p. 174 (photo g): GCShutter/E+/Getty Images; p. 32 (photo 3): stevecoleimages/E+/Getty Images; p. 32 (photo 4): Sam Edwards/Caiaimage/Getty Images; p. 33 (L): clearandtransparent/E+/Getty Images; p. 33 (RL), p. 38 (pack), p. 48 (TL, CL), p. 56 (Fatima), p. 68 (interesting), p. 69 (interesting), p. 70 (teeth), p. 100 (TC), p. 119 (hungry), p. 128 (photo 1.3): Hero Images/Getty Images; p. 33 (R), p. 36 (BCL), p. 46 (father), p. 48 (B), p. 50 (CL), p. 115, p. 156 (check-up), p. 162 (L), p. 179 (photo 3), p. 179 (photo 4), p. 182 (thinking): Katarina Premfors/arabianEye/Getty Images; p. 34 (TL), p. 46 (mother, brother), p. 100 (C), p. 106 (L), p. 112 (Huda, Tariq): visualspace/E+/Getty Images; p. 34 (TR): Eric Audras/ONOKY/Getty Images; p. 34 (BR), p. 174 (photo e): Nils Hendrik Mueller/Cultura/Getty Images; p. 36 (Saudi Arabian flag), p. 37 (Saudi Arabian flag), p. 38 (Saudi Arabian flag): Martin Konz/Hemera/Getty Images Plus/Getty Images; p. 36 (UK flag), p. 38 (UK flag): Nikola93/iStock/Getty Images Plus/Getty Images; p. 36 (Indian flag), p. 37 (Indian flag), p. 38 (Indian flag): Paper Boat Creative/Photodisc/Getty Images; p. 36 (Japanese flag), p. 37 (Japanese flag), p. 38 (Japanese flag), p. 57 (kite): Tetra Images/Getty Images; p. 36 (Bahraini flag), p. 38 (Bahraini flag), p. 144 (tablet): daboost/iStock/Getty Images Plus/Getty Images; p. 36 (Turkish flag), p. 38 (Turkish flag): colematt/iStock/Getty Images Plus/Getty Images; p. 36 (Portuguese flag), p. 37 (Portuguese flag), p. 38 (Portuguese flag): chelovek/iStock/Getty Images Plus/Getty Images; p. 36 (Mexican flag), p. 38 (Mexican flag): Veronaa/iStock/Getty Images Plus/Getty Images; p. 36 (BL): petekarici/iStock/Getty Images Plus/Getty Images; p. 36 (BCR): Thomas Fricke/Design Pics/Getty Images; p. 36 (BR), p. 49 (talking), p. 81 (photo 1.d): NicolasMcComber/E+/Getty Images; p. 37 (CL): aldomurillo/iStock/Getty Images Plus/Getty Images; p. 37 (CR), p. 93: Image Source/Stockbyte/Getty Images; p. 37 (B): gulfimages/Getty Images; p. 38 (T): Pedro Venâncio/EyeEm/Getty Images; p. 38 (bush): DAE/De Agostini/Getty Images; p. 38 (peas): James Galpin/Moment/Getty Images; p. 38 (bee): Michael Marsh/Moment/Getty Images; p. 38 (pill): TS Photography/Getty Images; p. 38 (bill): Peter Cade/The Image Bank/Getty Images; p. 38 (horse): Argijale/Moment/GettyImages; p. 38 (pear): Cube/Ikon Images/Getty Images; p. 38 (bear): Frans Lemmens/Corbis Unreleased/Getty Images; p. 38 (bin): Ryan McVay/Photodisc/Getty Images; p. 38 (pin): Atomic Imagery/DigitalVision/Getty Images; p. 39 (library card), p. 40 (library card): sd619/iStock/Getty Images Plus/Getty Images; p. 39 (ID card), p. 40 (ID card), 44 (photo e): jpgfactory/iStock/Getty Images Plus/Getty Images; p. 39 (pen), p. 40 (pen): Floortje/E+/Getty Images; p. 39 (pencil): Caziopeia/iStock/Getty Images Plus/Getty Images; p. 39 (Unlock), p. 62 (Unlock), p. 63 (Unlock): Cover from Book Unlock by Sabina Ostrowska; p. 39 (notebook), p. 40 (notebook): Hemera Technologies/PhotoObjects.net/Getty Images Plus/Getty Images; p. 39 (smartphone), p. 40 (smartphone), p. 142 (smartphone): scanrail/iStock/Getty Images Plus/Getty Images; p. 39 (dictionary), p. 40 (dictionary): Cover form Book Cambridge Essential dictionary; p. 40 (BL), p. 95 (manager): asiseeit/E+/Getty Images; p. 40 (BR): David Lees/DigitalVision/Getty Images Plus/Getty Images; p. 41 (hat), p. 57 (hat): penguenstok/E+/Getty Images; p. 41 (thermometer): VladisChern/iStock/Getty Images Plus/Getty Images; p. 41 (bill): Adam Gault/OJO Images/Getty Images; p. 41 (bell): Zoonar RF/Getty Images Plus/Getty Images; p. 41 (bag): LotusWorks/iStock/Getty Images Plus/Getty Images; p. 41 (bill): Adam Gault/OJO Images/Getty Images; p. 41 (desk): poligonchik/iStock/Getty Images Plus/Getty Images; p. 41 (disk), p. 176, 178 (photo 4): kyoshino/E+/Getty Images; p. 41 (man): Daly and Newton/OJO Images/Getty Images; p. 41 (bus): Andrew_Howe/E+/Getty Images; p. 44 (photo a): Taqwa Gad/EyeEm/Getty Images; p. 44 (photo c): Gary Conner/Stockbyte/Getty Images; p. 44 (photo d): Gajus/iStock/Getty Images Plus/Getty Images; p. 45, p. 47 (CR), p. 90 (TR): Hill Street Studios/Blend Images/Getty Images; p. 46 (grandfather, brother), p. 64, p. 110 (photo 1), p. 175, p. 188 (R): arabianEye/Getty Images; p. 46 (grandmother): Gogosvm/iStock/Getty Images Plus/Getty Images; p. 46 (father), p. 148 (photo c), p. 164 (photo 3), p. 182 (station): franckreporter/E+/Getty Images; p. 47 (R): AntonioGuillem/iStock/Getty Images Plus/Getty Images; p. 48 (TR): LWA/Larry Williams/Blend Images/Getty Images; p. 49 (TL): FrankvandenBergh/E+/Getty Images; p. 49 (TR): Aldo Murillo/iStock/Getty Images Plus/Getty Images;

Images; p. 102 (wash): skynesher/E+/Getty Images; p. 102 (fly): Martin Ruegner/Photographer's Choice/Getty Images; p. 103 (CR): CatLane/iStock/Getty Images Plus/Getty Images; p. 103 (BL): Stockbyte/Getty Images; p. 103 (BR): Aleksander Rubtsov/Blend Images/Getty Images; p. 105 (cloud): Frances Sutherland/EyeEm/Getty Images; p. 105 (house): irina88w/iStock/Getty Images Plus/Getty Images; p. 105 (pointing): Stanislaw Pytel/Taxi/Getty Images; p. 105 (mouth): moodboard/Cultura/Getty Images; p. 105 (pencil): MikLav/iStock/Getty Images Plus/Getty Images; p. 105 (coins): asafta/iStock/Getty Images Plus/Getty Images; p. 105 (boys): Leanne Temme/Photolibrary/Getty Images; p. 105 (shout): kupicoo/E+/Getty Images; p. 106 ©, p. 129 (TR): Monty Rakusen/Cultura/Getty Images; p. 106 (B), p. 179 (B): Niedring/Drentwett/MITO images/Getty Images; p. 108 (L): BernardaSv/iStock/Getty Images Plus/Getty Images; p. 108 (C): fizkes/iStock/Getty Images Plus/Getty Images; p. 108 (B), p. 183 (photo c): Flashpop/Iconica/Getty Images; p. 108: ZouZou1/iStock/Getty Images Plus/Getty Images; p. 110 (photo 3): Tevarak/iStock/Getty Images Plus/Getty Images; p. 110 (photo 4): George Coppock/Photolibrary/Getty Images; p. 110 (photo 5): pictafolio/E+/Getty Images; p. 110 (photo 6): franckreporter/iStock/Getty Images Plus/Getty Images; p. 110 (photo 7): billnoll/iStock/Getty Images Plus/Getty Images; p. 110 (photo 8): Takashi Sakata/Getty Images; p. 110 (photo 9): servet yigit/E+/Getty Images; p. 110 (photo 10): Andrew Bret Wallis/Stockbyte/Getty Images; p. 110 (photo 11): fcafotodigital/iStock/Getty Images Plus/Getty Images; p. 110 (photo 12): Magone/iStock/Getty Images Plus/Getty Images; p. 110 (photo 13): Rosemary Calvert/Photographer's Choice RF/Getty Images; p. 110 (photo 14): ovbelov/iStock/Getty Images Plus/GettyImages; p. 111 (photo 1): fcafotodigital/iStock/Getty Images Plus/GettyImages; p. 111 (photo 2): Andrew Bret Wallis/Stockbyte/GettyImages; p. 111 (photo 3): George Coppock/Photolibrary/GettyImages; p. 111 (photo 4): Andrew Unangst/Photographer's Choice/GettyImages; p. 112 (Natasha): Vivek Mukherjee Photography/Moment/Getty Images; p. 112 (photo 1): Gareth Morgans/StockFood Creative/Getty Images; p. 112 (photo 2): MilenaKatzer/iStock/Getty Images Plus/Getty Images; p. 112 (photo 3): millionsjoker/iStock/Getty Images Plus/Getty Images; p. 112 (photo 4): ALLEKO/iStock/Getty Images Plus/Getty Images; p. 112 (photo 5): Thomas Firak Photography/Photolibrary/Getty Images; p. 112 (photo 6): SerAlexVi/iStock/Getty Images Plus/Getty Images; p. 113 (photo 1): AVAVA/iStock/Getty Images Plus/Getty Images; p. 113 (photo 3): Monkey Business Images/Monkey Business/Getty Images Plus/Getty Images; p. 113 (photo 4): PeopleImages/E+/Getty Images; p. 113 (photo 6): Antonio_Diaz/iStock/Getty Images Plus/Getty Images; p. 113 (photo 7): sanjeri/E+/Getty Images; p. 113 (R): Gallo Images - Guy Bubb/Getty Images; p. 116 (photo 1): letty17/E+/Getty Images; p. 116 (photo 2): Lauri Rotko/Folio/Getty Images; p. 116 (photo 3): Brian Hagiwara/Photolibrary/Getty Images; p. 116 (photo 4): LatitudeStock - Stuart Pearce/Gallo Images/Getty Images; p. 116 (photo 5): tomazl/iStock/Getty Images Plus/Getty Images; p. 116 (photo 6): DAJ/Getty Images; p. 117: Kathrin Ziegler/Taxi/Getty Images; p. 118 (chips): Diana Miller/Cultura/Getty Images; p. 118 (cheese): Sean Gallup/Getty Images News/Getty Images; p. 118 (green tea): NatalyaTerr/iStock/Getty Images Plus/Getty Images; p. 119 (busy): Erik Dreyer/The Image Bank/Getty Images; p. 119 (great): Tempura/E+/Getty Images; p. 119 (well): Kirbyphoto/E+/Getty Images; p. 121 (coffee): jennyhorne/E+/Getty Images; p. 121 (tea): s-cphoto/E+/Getty Images; p. 121 (bank): Richard Cummins/Lonely Planet Images/Getty Images; p. 121 (ink): kemie/E+/Getty Images; p. 121 (plank): kyoshino/iStock/Getty Images Plus/Getty Images; p. 121 (car): braverabbit/iStock/Getty Images Plus/Getty Images; p. 121 (vest): s-cphoto/iStock/Getty Images Plus/Getty Images; p. 121 (January): jeangill/iStock/Getty Images Plus/Getty Images; p. 121 (book): spaxiax/iStock/Getty Images Plus/Getty Images; p. 121 (tree): Richard Gray/EyeEm/Getty Images; p. 121 (bench): Les Hirondelles Photography/Moment Open/Getty Images; p. 121 (cleaning)): Howard Shooter/Dorling Kindersley/Getty Images; p. 121 (link): BamBamImages/E+/Getty Images; p. 121 (tank): GK Hart/Vikki Hart/The Image Bank/Getty Images; p. 121 (list): ChristianChan/iStock/Getty Images Plus/Getty Images; p. 121 (mink): fotojagodka/iStock/Getty Images Plus/Getty Images; p. 121 (mist): Umar Shariff Photography/Moment Open/Getty Images; p. 121 (pinch): Gen Nishino/Photographer's Choice/Getty Images; p. 126 (photo 1): Pankaj & Insy Shah/Getty Images; p. 126 (photo 3): Salvator Barki/Gallo Images/Getty Images; p. 126 (photo 4): M Swiet Productions/Moment/Getty Images; p. 126 (photo 5): Jean-Pierre Lescourret/Lonely Planet Images/Getty Images; p. 126 (photo 6): Flashpop/Stone/Getty Images; p. 126 (photo 7): enviromantic/E+/Getty Images; p. 127 (TL): aydinmutlu/E+/Getty Images; p. 127 (TCL): Florian Trojer/Moment/Getty Images; p. 127 (TCR): Tony C French/Photolibrary/Getty Images; p. 127 (TR): BSIP/UIG/Universal Images Group/Getty Images; p. 127 (CL): Tim Robberts/The Image Bank/Getty Images; p. 127 (CCL): David Crespo/Moment/Getty Images; p. 127 (CCR): Frank Fell/robertharding/Getty Images; p. 127 (CL): Peter Durant/Arcaid Images/Arcaid Images/Getty Images; p. 128 (photo 1.1): JulNichols/iStock/Getty Images Plus/Getty Images; p. 128 (photo 1.2): Jay's photo/Moment/Getty Images; p. 128 (photo 1.4): fcafotodigital/E+/Getty Images; p. 128 (photo 1.5): Tom Merton/

Caiaimage/Getty Images; p. 128 (photo 1.6), p. 169 (park): Chris Clor/Blend Images/Getty Images; p. 128 (fort): Lizzie Shepherd/robertharding/Getty Images; p. 128 (fork): Jay's photo/Moment Open/Getty Images; p. 128 (pieces): Jorg Greuel/DigitalVision/Getty Images; p. 128 (park): Nikko Tee/EyeEm/Getty Images; p. 128 (court): ngkaki/iStock/Getty Images Plus/Getty Images; p. 128 (oil): Roman Kozlov/Hemera/Getty Images Plus/Getty Images; p. 129 (TL): ismagilov/iStock/Getty Images Plus/Getty Images; p. 129 (C): Topic Images Inc./Topic Images/Getty Images; p. 129 (CR): slava296/iStock/Getty Images Plus/Getty Images; p. 130: Angelo Cavalli/robertharding/robertharding/Getty Images; p. 131: RossHelen/iStock/Getty Images Plus/Getty Images; p. 132 (TL): Nickos/iStock/Getty Images Plus/Getty Images; p. 132 (TC): Jacek_Sopotnicki/iStock/Getty Images Plus/Getty Images; p. 132 (TR), p. 148 (photo b), p. 180 (dress): Peter Unger/Lonely Planet Images/Getty Images; p. 132 (CL): Sergio Parisi/Moment/Getty Images; p. 132 (C): Amaia Arozena & Gotzon Iraola/Moment Open/Getty Images; p. 132 (CR): Manuel Queimadelos Alonso/Getty Images Sport/Getty Images; p. 133 (photo 1): Astrakan Images/Cultura/Getty Images; p. 133 (photo 2): David Freund/Photolibrary/Getty Images; p. 133 (photo b): DEA/W. BUSS/De Agostini/Getty Images; p. 133 (photo f): Aitormmfoto/iStock Editorial/Getty Images Plus/Getty Images; p. 133 (photo e): Paul M O'Connell/Moment/Getty Images; p. 133 (photo d): Cultura RM Exclusive/Lost Horizon Images/Cultura Exclusive/Getty Images; p. 133 (photo c): Jon Arnold/AWL Images/Getty Images; p. 133 (B): Jason Hawkes/Getty Images News/Getty Images; p. 134: VitalyEdush/iStock/Getty Images Plus/Getty Images; p. 137 (station): Marcos Ferro/Aurora/Getty Images; p. 137 (train): LeoPatrizi/iStock/Getty Images Plus/Getty Images; p. 137 (street): Pinghung Chen/EyeEm/Getty Images; p. 137 (stairs): Glow Decor/Glow/Getty Images; p. 137 (star): chaofann/iStock/Getty Images Plus/Getty Images; p. 137 (tree): Liesel Bockl/Getty Images; p. 137 (traffic jam): Kichigin/iStock/Getty Images Plus/Getty Images; p. 137 (trolley): itsskin/E+/Getty Images; p. 137 (weight): ULU_BIRD/iStock/Getty Images Plus/Getty Images; p. 137 (string): fotyma/iStock/Getty Images Plus/Getty Images; p. 137 (arrow): LeonidKos/iStock/Getty Images Plus/Getty Images; p. 138 (L): Christian Kober/AWL Images/Getty Images; p. 138 (CL): Siddharth Siva/arabianEye/Getty Images; p. 138 (CR): alvarez/E+/Getty Images; p. 138 (R): Seongjoon Cho/Lonely Planet Images/Getty Images; p. 141: Gavin Hellier/AWL Images/Getty Images; p. 142 (laptop): Rouzes/iStock/Getty Images Plus/Getty Images; p. 142 (game): Manuel Breva Colmeiro/Moment Open/Getty Images; p. 142 (t-shirt): amriphoto/E+/Getty Images; p. 142 (newspaper): Bill Oxford/iStock/Getty Images Plus/Getty Images; p. 142 (bank card), p. 144 (bank card): ayo888/iStock/Getty Images Plus/Getty Images; p. 142 (watch): Mark Harwood/The Image Bank/Getty Images; p. 142 (tablet): Future Publishing/Future/Getty Images; p. 143 (watche): lucadp/iStock/Getty Images Plus/Getty Images; p. 143 (tablet): Apple Bookazine/Future/Getty Images; p. 143 (laptop): vladru/iStock/Getty Images Plus/Getty Images; p. 143 (t-shirts): conejota/iStock/Getty Images Plus/Getty Images; p. 144 (laptops): thumb/iStock/Getty Images Plus/Getty Images; p. 144 (t-shirts): sewer11/iStock/Getty Images Plus/Getty Images; p. 144 (watch): AlexandrMoroz/iStock/Getty Images Plus/Getty Images; p. 144 (smartphone): ET-ARTWORKS/iStock/Getty Images Plus/Getty Images; p. 146: zeynepogan/iStock/Getty Images Plus/Getty Images; p. 148 (photo 1), p. 166 (paper): Dougal Waters/DigitalVision/Getty Images; p. 148 (photo 2): Burazin/Photographer's Choice RF/Getty Images; p. 148 (photo 3), p. 148 (photo 5): BakiBG/iStock/Getty Images Plus/Getty Images; p. 148 (photo 4): Glow Images, Inc/Glow/Getty Images; p. 148 (photo a): Oktay Ortakcioglu/E+/Getty Images; p. 149 (photo 1): Evgeny Ermakov/iStock Editorial/Getty Images Plus/Getty Images; p. 149 (photo 2): flukyfluky/iStock/Getty Images Plus/Getty Images; p. 149 (photo 3), p. 185 (sleeping): Ridofranz/iStock/Getty Images Plus/Getty Images; p. 150 (payment): DGLimages/iStock/Getty Images Plus/Getty Images; p. 150 (tray): Glow Cuisine/Glow/Getty Images; p. 150 (playing): Alistair Berg/DigitalVision/Getty Images; p. 150 (chess): Alex Mares-Manton/Asia Images/Getty Images; p. 150 (face): Patrick LaRoque/First Light/Getty Images; p. 150 (tape): Coprid/iStock/Getty Images Plus/Getty Images; p. 150 (waving), p. 173: michaeljung/iStock/Getty Images Plus/Getty Images; p. 150 (chain): PM Images/DigitalVision/Getty Images; p. 150 (paint): Oleksiy Maksymenko/Getty Images; p. 150 (brain): Pixologicstudio/Science Photo Library/Getty Images; p. 150 (horse): Argijale/Moment/Getty Images; p. 151 (EUR): ©European Central Bank; p. 151 (USD): ©US Mint; p. 151 (GBP): ©The Royal Mint; p. 152 (B): LoooZaaa/iStock Editorial/Getty Images Plus/Getty Images; p. 153 (shopping): m-imagephotography/iStock/Getty Images Plus/Getty Images; p. 153 (bags): Martin Poole/DigitalVision/Getty Images; p. 153 (hand): deepblue4you/E+/Getty Images; p. 153 (shirt): Rubberball/Mike Kemp/Getty Images; p. 153 (trees): Jeff Greenberg/Universal Images Group/Getty Images; p. 153 (bird): Peter Garner/EyeEm/Getty Images; p. 153 (band): David Steele/Gallo Images/Getty Images; p. 153 (drum): tillsonburg/iStock/Getty Images Plus/Getty Images; p. 156 (running): Jetta Productions/DigitalVision/Getty Images; p. 156 (clothes): dvoevnore/iStock/Getty Images Plus/Getty Images; p. 156 (shoes): MVorobiev/iStock/Getty Images Plus/Getty Images; p. 156 (BG), p. 161 (Wi-Fi), p. 163 (Wi-Fi): goldy/iStock/Getty

Corpus

Development of this publication has made use of the Cambridge English Corpus (CEC). The CEC is a multi-billion word computer database of contemporary spoken and written English. It includes British English, American English, and other varieties of English. It also includes the Cambridge Learner Corpus, developed in collaboration with the University of Cambridge ESOL Examinations. Cambridge University Press has built up the CEC to provide evidence about language use that helps to produce better language teaching materials

Typeset by emc design ltd

EXTRA HANDWRITING NOTES

UNL⌀CK BASIC SKILLS
LAYING THE FOUNDATIONS FOR ACADEMIC SUCCESS

Unlock Basic Skills has been developed for pre-A1 learners. Combining the four skills with a focus on literacy and an introduction to critical thinking, students are supported as they set out on the path towards academic success.

What makes *Unlock Basic Skills* special:

- **Insights** gained from **expert teachers** ensure the course meets the specific academic needs of your pre-A1 students.

- Our **research** into over **5 million** words students use and need has informed the language taught in *Unlock Basic Skills*.

- **Listening, Speaking, Reading and Writing skills** are integrated within **academic contexts** to provide students with an effective and manageable learning experience.

- **Watch and remember** lessons in every unit include **video** and motivate students to **recycle and extend** the language they've learned.

- **An introduction to critical thinking skills** supports students in speaking and writing as they take their first steps to academic success.

A Teacher's Book with downloadable audio, video and Presentation Plus is also available.

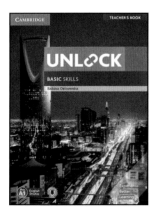

cambridge.org/unlock

UNL⚭CK LEVELS 1–4

BUILD ON YOUR STUDENTS' SUCCESS

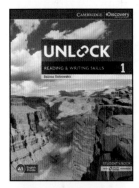

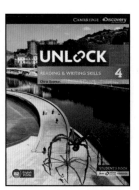

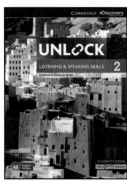

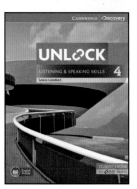

> *Unlock is the best textbook I have ever taught with. It contains a variety of topics that provide students with a wide range of vocabulary. Students are totally involved, which guarantees effective learning. Unlock helps to encourage and empower the students' critical thinking.*
>
> **Salima Al-Hadithi, Institute of Applied Technology, UAE**

Unlock Reading & Writing Skills	Level 1	Level 2	Level 3	Level 4
Student's Book with Online Workbook	978-1-107-61399-7	978-1-107-61400-0	978-1-107-61526-7	978-1-107-61525-0
Student's ebook with Online Workbook	978-1-107-65066-4	978-1-107-64409-0	978-1-107-63757-3	978-1-107-67139-3
Teacher's Book with DVD	978-1-107-61401-7	978-1-107-61403-1	978-1-107-61404-8	978-1-107-61409-3
Presentation Plus DVD-ROM	978-1-107-63800-6	978-1-107-65605-5	978-1-107-67624-4	978-1-107-68245-0
Unlock Listening & Speaking Skills	**Level 1**	**Level 2**	**Level 3**	**Level 4**
Student's Book with Online Workbook	978-1-107-67810-1	978-1-107-68232-0	978-1-107-68728-8	978-1-107-63461-9
Student's ebook with Online Workbook	978-1-107-67008-2	978-1-107-63562-3	978-1-107-67610-7	978-1-107-63710-8
Teacher's Book with DVD	978-1-107-66211-7	978-1-107-64280-5	978-1-107-68154-5	978-1-107-65052-7
Presentation Plus DVD-ROM	978-1-107-66424-1	978-1-107-69582-5	978-1-107-63543-2	978-1-107-64381-9